Trübner's Oriental Series

TSUNI-GOAM

Trübner's Oriental Series

AFRICA
In 3 Volumes

I   A Sketch of the Modern Languages of Africa Vol I
       Robert Needham Cust
II   A Sketch of the Modern Languages of Africa Vol II
       Robert Needham Cust
III   Tsuni-Goam
       Theophilus Hahn

TSUNI-GOAM

THE SUPREME BEING OF THE KHOI-KHOI

THEOPHILUS HAHN

LONDON AND NEW YORK

First published 1881 by
Trübner & Co Ltd

2 Park Square, Milton Park, Abingdon, Oxon OX14 4RN
711 Third Avenue, New York, NY 10017, USA

Transferred to Digital Printing 2007

Routledge is an imprint of the Taylor & Francis Group, an informa business

First issued in paperback 2016

Copyright © 1881 Theophilus Hahn

All rights reserved. No part of this book may be reprinted or reproduced or utilised in any form or by any electronic, mechanical, or other means, now known or hereafter invented, including photocopying and recording, or in any information storage or retrieval system, without permission in writing from the publishers.

Notice:
Product or corporate names may be trademarks or registered trademarks, and are used only for identification and explanation without intent to infringe.

The publishers have made every effort to contact authors/copyright holders of the works reprinted in *Trübner's Oriental Series*.
This has not been possible in every case, however, and we would welcome correspondence from those individuals/companies we have been unable to trace.

These reprints are taken from original copies of each book. In many cases the condition of these originals is not perfect. The publisher has gone to great lengths to ensure the quality of these reprints, but wishes to point out that certain characteristics of the original copies will, of necessity, be apparent in reprints thereof.

British Library Cataloguing in Publication Data
A CIP catalogue record for this book
is available from the British Library

Tsuni-Goam
ISBN 978-0-415-24455-8 (hbk)
ISBN 978-1-138-98621-3 (pbk)
Africa: 3 Volumes
ISBN 978-0-415-24283-7
Trübner's Oriental Series
ISBN 978-0-415-23188-6

TSUNI-‖GOAM

THE SUPREME BEING

OF THE

KHOI-KHOI

BY

THEOPHILUS HAHN, Ph.D.

CUSTODIAN OF THE GREY COLLECTION, CAPE TOWN;
CORRESP. MEMBER OF THE GEOGR. S. DRESDEN; CORRESP. MEMBER OF THE
ANTHROPOL. S. VIENNA, ETC. ETC.

LONDON
TRÜBNER & CO., LUDGATE HILL
1881

[All rights reserved]

TO

The Memory

OF

THE LATE

GEHEIMRATH HANS CONON VON DER GABELENTZ

OF POSCHWITZ

AND TO

PROFESSOR AUG. FRIEDR. POTT

OF HALLE ON THE SAALE

PREFACE.

THE following pages must speak for themselves; they will, I trust, be welcome to the student of Comparative Mythology, and to the Ethnologist and Anthropologist in general.

The reader will be sometimes disappointed on finding that my references to authorities are not always exact enough. I had often to quote from memory, and had then to confine myself to mentioning the names of the authors only. I may, however, expect that the reader will be lenient towards my failings on this point, if he puts himself in my position. I live here in a country village, and am entirely confined to my own small collection of books. The nearest and largest Colonial Library is in Cape Town, where, I am sorry to say, the standard works on Comparative Philology, Ethnology, and Anthropology, as well as the leading Journals and Periodicals of the Societies which cultivate these sciences, are still *desiderata*. With regard to Africa, and especially to South Africa, more and better selected materials are found in the Libraries of Vienna, Berlin, and London, than in the South African Public Library in Cape Town. The blame, however, does not attach to the Committee of Management, who indeed, with the limited means in their hands, have tried to please all parties. *Colonists have still to be taught to look on the South African Public Library as a National Institution, and with this view, in a true patriotic spirit, to contribute voluntarily such books, records, and documents as bear specially on our country.* Then, and then only, the South African Public Library will thrive as a public institution, and soon become the workshop and nursery of South African science. With the spread of education, no doubt the interest in "Our Library" will increase. The name of Dr. Dale, the Superintendent General of Education in this Colony, is a guarantee that education will continue to advance with daily greater strides; and thus we may hope that, ere long, Colonial youths will aspire to distinguish themselves in historical and purely philosophical studies.

For the orthography of the Hottentot and Bantu words, I employed, with slight modifications, the excellent Standard Alphabet of Professor Lepsius, which proves, after all, the most serviceable, as far as South African languages are concerned.

The words and names quoted from travellers are given in their own orthography; in a few instances, however, I considered it necessary to substitute for their spelling that introduced by Professor Lepsius, in order to render the phonetic composition of words more transparent, and, consequently, their etymology more evident. The clicks, which are of vital importance for the etymologist, are very indiscriminately treated by most travellers, with the sole exception of Professor Dr. Gustav Fritsch.

Travellers and missionaries who wish to serve the cause of South African Philology should be well acquainted with the principles of Phonology before they venture to write down texts of illiterate languages. No missionary should be sent to the heathens without having acquired as thorough a knowledge of Phonetics as he has of the Gospel, and he should be taught to respect every vowel, every accent, every consonant; in fact, "*every jot and tittle in any, even the most barbarous, dialect he may hereafter have to analyse.*"[*] Comparative Philology is entirely based upon phonology, and if the laws of phonology for a group of languages are

[*] Max Müller, "Lect." ii. p. 42, ed. 1868.

once correctly established, the natural offshoot will be a true scientific etymology. This science is *the* telescope with which, where all other records fail, we can draw prehistoric times into our immediate view, and which allows us a look far back into " the very dawn of man's life."

It is an urgent want for us here in South Africa that a Standard Orthography for the Native Languages should be introduced in all official, educational, and public departments. The task is not as difficult as it may appear at first sight, and where there is a will, there is a way.

In the present Standard Orthography we write the clicks as follows:—

The Lateral ||, [1] ||a, [2] ||na, [3] ||khā, [4] ||ga,
The Cerebral |, [5] |ā, [6] |nā, [7] |khā, [8] |gā,
The Palatal ‡, [9] ‡ā, [10] ‡nā, [11] ‡khā, [12] ‡ga.
The Dental |, [13] |ā, [14] |nā, [15] |khā, [16] |gā.

The importance of the clicks will be best illustrated by giving the meanings of these words here at once, thus, [1] to wash, [2] to drop, [3] to be able, [4] to split, [5] to fall, [6] to light, [7] to bore, to perforate, [8] to serve, [9] to wash, [10] to pour, [11] to refuse, [12] to plant, [13] to be sharp, [14] to filter, [15] with, [16] isolated, separated, thin, &c., dotted.

Those who wish to inform themselves about the nature of these clicks and their bearing on the phonology of the Hottentot language, I refer to Henry Tindall's excellent " Grammar and Vocabulary of the Namaqua-Hottentot Language," and to my " Sprache der Nama."

In Tindall's book, however, and in my own no mention is made of a harsh faucal sound peculiar to the old Cape Hottentot dialects—of which Witsen and Leibniz have supplied some materials—to the |Kora-Hottentot and to the Bushman languages of the |Kham, |Ai, |Nuni, |Koang, Hei‡guis, Matsanakhoi and |Gabe. I write this consonant, which most resembles a forcibly produced *short croaking sound*—just as if a person is endeavouring to get rid of a bone in the throat—with the Hebrew ȝ (ajin). *The very fact that this sound is produced by expiration and not by inspiration places it among the consonants proper, and not among the clicks.*

Most of the materials contained in this treatise have steadily accumulated during the last nine years. Aware of the responsibility resting upon me, I have been careful to adduce such facts only as I can with full confidence declare to be genuine productions of the Khoikhoi mind.

The following pages were written down in their present shape in the months of August and September last year, as is known to Professors Max Müller, of Oxford, and Friedrich Müller, of Vienna, and other friends to whom I either wrote or spoke on the subject at the time.[†]

I mention this the more as to-day a copy of the *Ausland*, February 16, 1880, comes to my hands, in which an article, Die Religion der sogenan ten Wilden, reviewing Gustav Roskoff's book, "Das Religionswesen der rohesten Naturvölker," Leipzig, 1880, contains views and opinions coinciding so strikingly with those expressed by me, that the reader could easily be led to believe that either I must have perused Professor Roskoff's work, or that he had corresponded with me. This, however, is not the case, and therefore this peculiar coincidence may serve as a striking evidence of what I say, towards the conclusion of the third chapter, about the *psychical identity of the human mind*. At the same time it is a great satisfaction and encouragement to find that one does not stand alone with his views, and that there are comrades and fellow-labourers in the battle-field, where one least expected them.

I desire to inscribe these leaves to the memory of the late Herr Geheimrath Hans Conon von der Gabelentz, and to Professor August Friedrich Pott, of Halle. These scholars will always be mentioned first in the history of

---

[*] Vide Theoph. Hahn, "Sprache der Nama," § 2, &c.
[†] The full manuscript was read over to my friends Profs. Walker and Marais of Stellenbosch.

South African Philology, as the pioneers who laid the foundation-stone of the Comparative Grammar of the Kafir-Congo or Bantu Languages.* Whatever has been written afterwards on Bantu Grammar, is based on the researches of these twin-stars in the realm of the Science of Language. In availing myself of this opportunity I simply pay a debt of gratitude. I was so fortunate as to have Professor Pott as my master and foster-father in the Science of Language for nearly four years, while I studied at the University of Halle, and my holidays were often spent at Poschwitz, the castle of Herr von der Gabelentz, where I had free access to his excellent African library.

Last, but not least, I have to tender my sincere obligations to Professor Max Müller for undertaking so kindly to see this treatise through the press.

THEOPHILUS HAHN.

STELLENBOSCH, CAPE OF GOOD HOPE,
March 24, 1880.

---

* Pott, Die Sprachen vom Kaffer und Kongostamme, in *Zeitschrift der D. M. Gesellschaft*, ii. 5-26, 129-158; and H. C. v. d. Gabelentz, in the "Proceedings" of the same Society, i. 241, seq.

TSŨI-‖GOAB.

CHAPTER I.

The facts of language, however small, are historical facts.—
MAX MÜLLER.

INTRODUCTORY REMARKS ON THE ETHNICAL CONDITION OF THE KHOIKHOI IN PREHISTORIC TIMES, BASED ON THE EVIDENCE OF LANGUAGE.

THE Khoikhoi form a branch of the most peculiar and, doubtless, of the most interesting race of all the representatives of mankind on our continent. These Khoikhoi generally go by the name of *Hottentots*, a term to which I must object, as up to this moment it has been the cause of gross misunderstanding and heartburning, especially to ethnologists, when they had in view the classification of the South African races and nations.

In order to introduce to the reader the worshippers of ¹Tsũi-‖goab and to lay a secure basis for the study of the Science of Religion as regards the ²Khoikhoi branch, I shall endeavour in a short sketch to delineate their prehistoric ethnical condition.

When the first European navigators, especially the Dutch, became acquainted with the Cape of Good Hope, they found a yellowish race of men, who possessed large herds of ³cattle, sheep and goats, and were on the whole, even after they had received a very provoking treatment at the hands of the Europeans, peaceably and ⁴hospitably inclined towards strangers. On account of their curious language abounding in harsh faucal sounds and clicks, the Dutch called them Hottentots. Hottentot or ⁵Hütten-tüt means in Frisian or Low German a quack, and therefore the old Dutchmen, who were so much puzzled and did not know what to make of such an unheard-of language, more akin to the chat of a parrot than to human speech, called it Hottentot—*i.e.*, a mere gibberish. They very little knew that they had before themselves a highly-developed language, so highly, indeed, that the ingenious Martin Haug supposes that its higher and more refined constituents must have been acquired by contact with a civilized people.

The old Dutch also did not know that their so-called Hottentots formed only one branch of a wide-spread race, of which the other branch divided into ever so many tribes, differing from each other totally in language, and having only a phonetic relationship, as regards certain peculiar sounds, of which the clicks formed the essential part. This other branch differed also entirely in language from those the Dutch had met first. · While the so-called Hottentots called themselves Khoikhoi (men of men, *i.e.*, men *par excellence*), they called those other tribes Sā, the Sonqua of the Cape Records.

This yellow race, consisting of these two branches, inhabited in ancient times the greater part of South Africa, at least the territory south of the rivers ⁶ Kunéne and Zambesi.

The appellation Hottentot is now *en vogue*, and as Goethe has it:—

"Wo die Begriffe fehlen,
Da stellt ein Wort zur rechten Zeit sich ein."
(For there precisely, where ideas fail,
A word comes in most opportunely.)

It is useless therefore to extirpate it, for the custom of more than two centuries has sanctioned its use ; and all we can do is to define it more accurately. We should apply the term *Hottentot* to the whole race, and call the two families, each by the native name, that is the one, the *Khoikhoi*, the so-called *Hottentot proper* ; the other the *Sān (Sā) or Bushmen.*

In the Nama language, one of the Khoikhoi idioms, the Bushmen are called Sā-n (com. plur). The meaning of this term is not quite intelligible, and I frankly confess that, after nine years, of which I have spent nearly seven amongst the Khoikhoi, I did not succeed in arriving at a quite satisfactory etymology, and I must still adhere to the interpretation which I first gave in the *Globus*, 1870, where I traced the word Sā-(b) to the root SÄ, to inhabit, to be located, to dwell, to be settled, to be quiet. Sā(n) consequently would mean Aborigines or Settlers proper. These Sa-n or Sa-gu-a, Sonqua or Sounqua, &c. (obj. plur. msc.) as they are styled in the Cape Records, are often called Bushmen—the Bossiesman, Bosjesman, Bosmanneken of the Colonial Annals, a name given to them to indicate their abode and mode of living.

The word Sā(b) has also acquired a low meaning, and is not considered to be very complimentary. The Khoikhoi often speak of |*Uri-Sān* (white Bushmen) and mean the low white vagabonds and runaway sailors who visit their country as traders. One also often hears, "*Khoikhoi tamab, Sab ke*," he is no Khoikhoi, he is a Sā, which means to say, "*he is no gentleman, he is of low extraction, or he is a rascal.*" A Nama will say of a man who is very proud and reserved in his manners, who only mixes in good society, "*Khoikhoisen ra aob ke*," the man *makes-a-Khoikhoi-of-himself*, that is, *he stands very much upon his dignity*, and also, *he keeps himself very much to himself.*

Those who desire to have information on the natural and physical condition of the Khoikhoi and Sā-(n), I refer to Dr. Gustav Fritsch's standard work, "Die Eingeborenen Süd-Africas," and to three Essays published by me, Die Namas, and Die Buschmänner, in the

Globus, 1868 and 1870, and Beiträge zur Kunde der Hottentoten, in *Jahresbericht des Vereins für Erdkunde,* Dresden, 1868 ; not to forget the chapter on the Hottentots in Friedr. Müller's excellent work "Allgemeine Ethnographie."

It is enough meanwhile to say, that the Bushmen lead the life of a Pariah, and that they are hated and chased by all other nations of South Africa, having to suffer most, however, from the hands of their own nearest kith and kin, the Khoikhoi, whom I have, on more than one occasion, seen manifesting more charity for a dog than for a starving Bushman.

The Khoikhoi are generally called, as I have already said, Hottentots, a term to which I would not object, were it not for the confusion it generally brings in its train, as far as ethnological, anthropological or linguistic terminology is concerned. Sometimes they are called the *Hottentots proper* in our Colonial language. But very often, again, our Khoikhoi in the Colony, or more particularly those remnants of the tribes formerly occupying the vicinity of Cape Town, are called *Hottentots, Hottentots proper* or *Cape Hottentots,* while on the other hand the inhabitants of Griqualand West, of the South Kalihari, of Great Namaqualand are called by their tribal names, Griquas, Namaquas, !Koras or Koranas, just as if they were not Hottentots as much as the Khoikhoi tribes of the Cape Colony. It would be as absurd for us to call only the Prussians, Germans, and apply to all the other tribes of Germany their tribal names, Bavarians, Suabians, Hessians, &c., denying to them the attribute German; or for Londoners to claim for themselves the title of Englishmen, while excluding the Northumberland and Sussex men from it.

This is my reason for protesting emphatically against the indiscriminate and superficial use of the term *Hottentot,* and therefore I have taken the liberty of taxing the patience of my readers by dwelling at some length on this subject.

While the Bushmen are hunters, the Khoikhoi are nomads, cattle and sheep farmers; and while the Bushman family has with the Khoikhoi, linguistically speaking, only the clicks and some harsh sounding faucals and a few roots of words in common, the various Bushman languages hitherto recorded, differ among themselves, as much as they differ from the Khoikhoi idioms. This difference and variety in speech is mainly due to their wandering habits and unsettled life. The wild inaccessible mountain strongholds and the arid deserts of South Africa, where nobody can follow them, are their abode; constantly on the alert, constantly on the move, constantly on the path of war, either with other tribes, or with the wild animals, no inducement is given to them for a settled life, the necessary condition of the development of a more articulate speech and a higher intellectual culture.

The Khoikhoi, or Nomadic Hottentots, have all the same language, which branches off in as many idioms and dialects as there are tribes. The idiomatic peculiarities, however, are not very prominent, indeed not so striking, as to hinder a Gei‖khau or ‡Auni or ‖Habobe of Great Namaqualand, and the ‡Nūbe of Ovambóland, or the Gei‡nam of the North Western Kalihari, conversing easily with the inhabitants of the Khamies Bergen (North Western Colony), and with the |Koras and Griquas of Griqualand West and the Orange Free State.

A prominent feature in all the *Khoikhoi* idioms is the strict monosyllabism of the root, ending in a vowel, and the use of pronominal elements as suffixes for the purpose of forming derivatives. The Khoikhoi language is entirely void of prefixes, nay, our prepositions are postpositions. The pronominal elements have in the course of time crystallized, and sometimes melted together into one, and in this new shape accepted the office of classifiers and registrars of substantives or substantified expressions, so that some of our most eminent philologists did not hesitate to consider them homogeneous with the article of other sex-denoting languages, chiefly of the Semitic and Hamitic class. But I am convinced that a more careful investigation will lead to the result, that the Khoikhoi language is not sex-denoting in the sense of Aryan or Semitic grammar. The so-called "*article*" is not an article in the sense of grammar, because the root of the Khoikhoi article is not the same throughout the genders, nor throughout the numbers. The following Table will at once explain what I mean:

		Masc.	Fem.	Com.
Sing.	Subjective	b (bi), m (mi)	s (si)	i
	Objective	ba, ma	sa	(ia) e
Dual.		Subj. and obj. khā	ra	ra
Plur.	Subjective	gu	ti	n
	Objective	ga (gua)	te (tia)	na

In saying this I do not for a single moment deny that the so-called article was *en route* to develop into the meaning and sense of the Aryan article, when by the destructive contact with other races—the Bantu from the North, and the European from the South—this development was suddenly checked.

We may therefore safely, until a more appropriate term for this way of classifying is established, call those particles which serve as classifiers of the three classes of the substantives, *Articles*.

The Bushman languages, as far as I had an opportunity of becoming acquainted with them, have no such derivative and formative elements; at least, if they had, such have now entirely disappeared, or are distorted to such a degree, that they defy every analysis. Sometimes one is tempted to believe that there are embryonic indications of such elements; sometimes again one is strongly inclined to take such would-be-suffixes, for dilapidated remnants of pronominal elements. The present Bushman languages bear nearly the same relationship to the Khoikhoi as, among the Indo-European languages, English holds to

Sanskrit. As to the dictionary of Khoikhoi and Bushman, there remains no more doubt as to their primitive relationship. The following list will convince the greatest sceptic:—

	Khoikhoi.	ǃKham-Bushman.
Tooth	ǁgūb	ǁgēi-ǁgeī
Intestines	ǀguin	ǀkhoin-ǀkhoin
Male, man	yau (ǃKora) au (Nama)	yau
Master	gao-yau-b (ǃKora)	gao-yau
Rope	ǀhaŭb	ǀhaŭ
Elephant	ǂkχoab	ǂkχoa
Egg	ǀubu-s	ǀubu and ǀuiten
Fish	ǁoub	ǁou
White	ǀuri	ǀuiten and ǀū
Star	ǀgomrob (ǃKora) ǀgamirob (Nama)	ǀkoaten
Plain	ǀoub	ǀougen
Strong	ǀgeiχa	ǀgeiya
Weak	ǂkχabu	ǂkχoba
Rich	ǃkχū	ǃkχou
Buchu	sāb	tsā
Beads	ǀurin (ǀyuri)	ǀyuri
Other	ǀkhara	ǀkχara
Selfsame	ǁeī	ǁeī
To walk	dā	taī
Clay	ǂgoa-b	ǂgoai
Sea	huri-b	huri
Interrog.	tari	tari

Or if we like to glance at the ǃAi-Bushman on the Northwest Kalihari, we shall come to the same conclusion.

	Khoikhoi.	ǃAi-Bushman.
Man	khoi-b	khoe
Male	yaore khoi-m (ǃKora)	yau-khoe
Child	ǀgŏa-ï	ǀgoa
Father	ǁgŭ-khoib	ǁgŭ-khoe

	Khoikhoi.	ǀAi-Bushman.
Cattle	go-ma-ï	goe
Calf	tsaŭ-b	tsaŭ
Sheep	gu-ï	gu
Goat	biri-ï	biri
Lion	χa-mi	χam
Dog	ari-b	arigu
Hare	ǀoa-ï	ǀoa
Hartebēst	ǁkhama-ï	ǁkhama
Nose	ǂgui-s	ǂgui
Mouth	ɥam-s (ǀKora)	ɥam
Tooth	ǁgŭ-b	ǁgŭ
Ear	ǂgeis	ǂgē
Arm	ǁoã-b	ǁoã
Neck	ǀɥaub (ǀKora)	ǀɥau
Leg	tĕ-b	tĕ
Tree	hei-ï	hiï
Beard	ǀnum-s	ǀnom
Hard	ǃgari	ǃgadi
Black	ǂnū	ǂnū
White	ǃuri	ǃū
To run	ǃgŭ	ǃgŭ
To drink	{ ɥā (ǀKora) ā (Nama) }	ɥā
To eat	ǂũ	ǂũ
To die	ǁō	ǁō
To give	mā	māme
To catch	ǃkhō	ǃkhō
Cap	ǀgabá-s	ǀgabá
Pot	sū-s	sū
Jackal	ǀgiri-b	ǀgirì
Bull	ǁgo-b	ǁgō
Fish	ǁou-b	ǁou
Snake	ǀɥau-b (ǀKora)	ǀɥau
Rain	tū-s	tū
Road	dao-b	dao
Fat	ǁnui-b	ǁnui

	Khoikhoi.	!Ai-Bushman.
Milk	bi-s	bi
Honey	dani-s (dini-s)	dini
Fly	ǀgina-s	ǀgini
Light	subu	subu
To laugh	yaī (ǃKora)	yaī
To see	mũ	mũ
To kiss	ǁoa	ǁobe

It is of vital importance that the roots, especially in the first syllables and clicks (Anlaut), should agree; and this is here the case.

A prominent feature in all Khoikhoi dialects is a strict monosyllabic tendency, and all roots end with a vowel, and chiefly with *a, i, u; e* and *o* are contractions of the three primitive vowels. As regards the roots in the Bushman languages, they appear more or less polysyllabic, although a great number is monosyllabic. They end generally in a vowel, very often also in a very strong nasal ~, which I believe is an old crippled suffix, originally having a vowel at the end. For instance, ǃgũ, to go, is by some pronounced ǃgun (ǃgung); this n, as can be proved, is contracted from nīge or nī-ge-ni. These vowels, however, have gradually worn off. Those roots which appear to be polysyllabic, very likely after a more careful study will prove to be compounds of radical elements.

While the Khoikhoi dialects all agree in having the same suffixes for the forming of three distinct numbers, (sing., dual, plur.) the Bushman languages show great irregularities and departures from the rule in this respect. In the ǀKham language (Northern Colonial Border about Kenhardt and Zakrevier)—*mirabile dictu*—the words *man* ǀ*kui goai*, and *woman* ǀ*kui* ǀ*aití*, differ even in the root entirely from the plural *men,* ǀ*ēga túgẹn,* and *women* ǀ*ēga* ǀ*gāgẹn*. They can therefore not be styled plurals in the general sense of the word.

Then again the plural will be formed simply by reduplication; but it also must be said that some individuals of the same tribe do not form a plural at all from the same word, where another individual would do so. There is also a goodly number of substantives, which are not used in the plural, because they are of a collective nature. A dual exists only for the first personal pronoun.

As regards the numerals, it seems that the Bushmen languages have not developed them beyond *two*; some travellers speak of *three*; but this is evidently derived from the Khoikhoi word ǃnora or ǃnona for *those*.

The ǀAi-Bushmen, however, who inhabit the North Western Kalihari in the neighbourhood of Xaïtsēs, (west from Lake Ngami or Nǁgami) count up to twenty, and for the sake of completeness I give these numerals here, as I have written them down from the mouth of three individuals of the ǀAi tribe.

	ǀAi-Bushman.	*Khoikhoi.*
One	ǀguïi	ǀgui
Two	ǀgam	ǀgam
Three	ǃnona	ǃnona
Four	geië	haga
Five	ǀguim tsoum (*i.e.*, one hand)	gore
Six	ǀguisa	ǃnani
Seven	ǀgamana	hũ (hũgu)
Eight	ǃnonadi	ǁkhaisa
Nine	ǀuitaï ǁgam	khoisi
Ten	ǁyaïko	disi
Eleven	tamkhumtsũ	disi ǀgui ǃkha
Twelve	ǀgamané	„ ǀgam „
Thirteen	ǃnonané	„ ǃnona „
Fourteen	ǁkheïsa	, haga „
Fifteen	tsũba ǁyāe	&c. &c.
Sixteen	ǀgui naha ǂgana	
Seventeen	ǀgam naha ǂgana	
Eighteen	ǃnona naha ǂgana	
Nineteen	ǀgamsaragásara	
Twenty	tsutsarukēhã	

I was so struck with the novelty of this discovery, in finding a Bushman tribe which could count beyond three, that I repeatedly cross-examined those individuals separately. I however still maintain the suspicion that this system of numerals is not genuine Bushman counting, but that we have to ascribe it to the influence of the neighbouring Bakoba tribes of the Touga River, or to the influence of the Mashona of the Lake n‖Gami, who often used to extend their hunting expeditions westward as far as Xaïtses (Ghanze of Galton) and even to the jungles of ∣Khunobis (Tunobis of Galton and Anderson).

A remarkable feature of the Khoikhoi language is the decimal system of counting; a system not adopted from the Europeans, but which was established long before the Khoikhoi or Nomadic Hottentot branch split into tribes, and spread over the various parts of South Africa, as will be seen from the following schedule taken from various authors who lived and travelled among the different Khoikhoi tribes at different times:—

	Witsen. Cape. 1691.	*Leibniz. Collect.* 1717.	*Valentyn. Cape.* 1705.
I.	K'qui	—	kchui
II.	K'kam	t ? amma	k-ham
III.	K'ouna	houna	n hona
IV.	Hacka	haka	hoka
V.	Kro	koro	kourou
VI.	Nanni	nani	nanni
VII.	Honcko	honko	honku
VIII.	K'hyssi	k ? heissee	kheyssi
IX.	K'geessi	guissi	ghesi
X.	Guissi	gissi	gissi

	Kolb. Cape. 1719.	*Barrow. Eastern.* 1797.	*Liechtenstein.* ∣*Kora.* 1805.
I.	G'kui	quai	t'koei
II.	K'kam	kam	t'kam
III.	K'ouna	gona	t'norra

Kolb. Cape.	Barrow. Eastern.	Liechtenstein. ǃKora.
1719.	1797.	1805.
IV. Hakka	haka	hakka
V. Koro	gose	kurruh
VI, Nanni	—	t'nani
VII. Honko	—	honko
VIII. Khyssi	—	t'kaissee
IX. K'hessi	—	t'goissee
X. Gyssi	—	diissi

	Alexander.	Knudsen.
Schmelen.	Great	Great
North-west Colony.	Namaqualand.	Namaqualand.
1814.	1834.	1842.
I. Goei	'kooe	˙gui
II. Kam	'tam	˙gam
III. Nona	'oona	"nona
IV. Haka	haka	haka
V. Kore	kore	gore
VI. Nanni	'nanee	"nani
VII. Hũ	hoo	*hu
VIII. 'Kysa	'keisa	'khaise
IX. Koisi	koësé	khoise
X. Disi	deesee	disi

Vollmer.	Tindall.	Th. Hahn.
Great Namaqualand.	N.E. Namaqualand.	Cape Town.
Red Nation.	Wesley Vale.	ǃKora Captive
1856.	1852.	1871.
I. ǀGui	ckui	ǀgui
II. ǀGam	ckam	ǀgama
III. ǂNona	qnona	ǀnona
IV. Haga	haka	haka
V. Goro	kore	koro
VI. ǂNani	qnani	ǀnani
VII. Hũ	hu	hongu
VIII. ǁKhaisa	xkhaisi	ǁkhaisa
XI. Khoisi	goisi	kχoisi
X. Disi	disi	dyisi

Th. Hahn. Oudtshoorn, E. Prov. 1871.	Th. Hahn. Bergdamara, North Namaqualand. 1875.
I. ǀKui	ǀkui
II. ǀKam	ǀkam
III. ǀNona	ǀnona
IV. Haka	haga
V. Koro	gore
VI. ǀNani	ǀnani
VII. Hŭgu	hŭ
VIII. ǁKhaisi	ǁkhaisa
IX. Khoisi	khoise
X. Disi	disi

A ǂNuwi-Namaqua from the Kaokoveldt counted in the same way as the Great Namaquas.

This much we know of the time when the numerals were formed, that it must have followed the period when the Khoikhoi family had left the isolating stage, and their language availed itself of the aid of pronominal elements in order to form derivatives ǀGui, ǀga-m, ǀno-na, ha-ga, go-re, ǀna-ni, hŭ-gu or hŭ-ni-gu, ǁkhai-si, khoi-si, di-si, all have the derivative-pronominal-suffixes, i, m, na, ni, gu, ga, re, si. We also know that the Khoikhoi could not have invented the numerals before their domestic and social condition made counting and taxing necessary. As long as they were hunters, there was nothing worth counting, but when they had taken to breeding cattle and sheep, they had to count (ǃgõa) their flocks, and the richest man was the most honoured man. Hence it is that ǃgõa, *to count*, is also used in the meaning, *to honour, to respect*, and ǃgõab means not only *the number*, but also *the honour, the respect, the regard*. "ǃGõahe tamata hã," will a Khoikhoi indignantly say, "I am not counted," that is, "I am not looked at," if he thinks that he is unfairly treated.

The meanings of some of these numerals are very clear. ǀGui, *one*, is the *single*, the *lonely* one. For instance, to know whether a man is by himself, one would ask, ǀGuriseb hã ? Is he alone ?

ǀGam, *two*, I derive from the root ǀka, ǀkha, ǀga, or ǀya, which is originally a post-position, meaning *with*, " *added*," " *contributed*," *in connection with*.

ǀNona, *three*, comes from ǀno-na-s or ǀno-ma-s, the *root*, the *radix* of a tree. In every plant the central root is the radical and strongest root. The same, the middle finger of every hand being the *root-finger*, it is obvious that this finger should have provided the name for the number *three*, because the natives count with the aid of the fingers; and whether they commence with the thumb or with the little finger, the central or middle finger always will turn out to be the *third* finger, and thus this finger became the symbol of the abstract number *three*.

Haga, four, I cannot venture to explain.

More interesting again is the derivation of *gore, five*, which means nothing else than the palm of the hand. The word *goreb*, for palm of the hand, is antiquated but still in use. I once told a girl to take a dish of food to her mother in return for milk which I had received, and told her to be careful and not to break the dish. She answered, "*Goreb* ǀna ta ni tani" (I will carry it in the palm of my hand). This is the way in which the Khoikhoi girls always carry their milk-vessels. 'Goreb is also the Euphorbia candelabra, and shows at the distance the profile or appearance of a vertically stretched arm with the open hand. It is certain that both the number *gore* and the *gore*-tree have derived the name from goreb (also koreb), the open hand. It is also certain that the number *gore* and the tree *kore* both are of the same age. The bark of this *gore*-tree has served from the earliest times as the chief material for the manufacturing of the quiver. Places have received their names from the abundance of these trees. There is a Koreχas in the North-western Cape Colony; a ǀKora told me that he was born at Koreχas in the Free State;

another Koreχas is in the |Gami-ǂnus territory in Southern Namaqualand, and another Koreχas in the Northwestern Kalihari, between Gobabis and Ghanze. It is well known that the Euphorbia candelabra shows the most beautiful and gigantic forms in the Khalamba Mountains and in Sekukuni's country and the Hoogeveldt (Highlands) of the Eastern Transvaal. From this we may conclude, as the *gore*-tree does not grow in flats, but is, in very few exceptions, almost entirely confined to mountainous territories, that the Khoikhoi before they separated lived in a mountainous country. This circumstance allows us to account for the higher development which they received before their cousins, the Bushmen. It also points out to us the primordial " fatherland" of the Khoikhoi.

We come now to the number |nani, *six*, where I am not able to give a satisfactory explanation.

Hŭ or *hŭyu* (originally *hunigu*) mean the " mixed ones," the " amalgamated ones," from *huni*, to stir, to amalgamate. For instance, if milk is thrown into coffee, a man says, " Hunire eibe ots ni |gāise ā." " Stir at first " (that is, mix the coffee with the milk), " and you will drink nicely." Whether here the seven colours of the rainbow gradually flowing into one another originated the idea of the number seven I cannot tell, but I think it possible.

||*Khaisi* or ||*khaisa, eight*, is very clear from the root ||*khai*, to turn ; thus ||khaisi means " turning number"—*i.e.*, four is turning back again.

Khoisi, nine, is not intelligible. All I can say is, that it has with *khoib*, man, the root *khoi* in common.

Disi, ten, from *di*, to do, would give us the meaning " done," " finished." And the Khoikhoi now continued *eleven*, disi-|gui-|kha ; twelve, disi-|gam-|kha—that is, ten-one-with, ten-two-with, &c. &c., or simply with striking off disi, ten, |gam-|kha, two-with, and so forth. Twenty is |gam disi, two tens ; thirty is !nona disi, three tens, &c. Hundred, disi disi, ten tens, or gei disi, great ten. For thousand, ǀoa gei disi, full-great-ten, is now in use, but I am not in the position to decide whether it is of very recent date or not.

If we had nothing else but these numerals, it would be enough to excite our admiration for the intellectual achievements of the pre-historic Khoikhoi. These numerals are the oldest records of philosophical thinking among the Redmen, and rank their inventors with the ancestors of our own Aryan race *as far as mental power is concerned*. But fortunately there are some more fragments and relics which open to us a clear view into the social, domestic, and religious daily life of the primitive Khoikhoi. He was a Nomad, and possessed large herds of cattle and sheep. The cattle (*gomán*) and sheep (*gūn*) were his riches ($\chi \bar{u}n$). A rich man (gou-aob) was a fat man; he could afford to be fat (*gousa*), he could anoint himself with fat (*goub*). Therefore the word *gou-aob, fat-man*, is identical with ǃkhū-aob, *rich-man*, and both have now become the words by which rulers, kings, chiefs, masters, and lords are addressed; gou-aob, or gao-aub, being generally used for chief or king, and ǃkhu-aob for master or lord, sometimes simply ǃkhūb, in which form it is also used for the "*Lord in heaven.*"

Naturally the richest man had the largest family, he could afford to buy wives as many as he liked; to love, to court, is ǁā, originally ǁama, which fuller form is still in use for *to buy, to barter*. This shows that the Khoikhoi bought their wives, and there must have been a remembrance of that custom still, when they first came in contact with the black Bantu races; for the Zulus have the same word ǁama for marrying—viz., buying a wife, a word which, from its click, shows the Khoikhoi origin.

It is now clear that the richest man became the most influential man, and gradually rose to the station of a chief. He could buy as many wives as he liked, and thus ruled through the number of relations and such admirers who had to live on him. It is now still expected that a Khoikhoi chief must have an open hand and an open house; and the worst that can be said of a chief is, that he is *gei-||are*—*i.e., greatly-lefthanded* or *stingy*. It happens sometimes, that another man is made chief, who is expected to be more liberal.

It was a great event in the history of the Hottentot language, when |*Guri-Khoisib*, the ancestor of the present nomadic Hottentots called himself the "Only-man," or *khoikhoib*, the man of men—*i.e.*, man *par excellence*; when he formed from the root *khoi* such abstract words as *khoisi*, friendly, human; *khoisis*, humanity, friendliness, kindness, friendship, or *khoiχa* and *khoiχasis*, kind and kindliness; *khoisigagus*, marriage, intimacy, friendship; *khoiχakhoib*, most intimate friend, or, as we say in German, *Herzensfreund*.

There is, indeed, a great and striking difference between the feelings and ideas of a Bushman and a Khoikhoi.

This word Khoikhoi opens to us another page of the records of the pre-historic Hottentots. It proves that besides the Sān or Bushmen, there were no other nations known to the Khoikhoi. The present Bergdamaras are called *Dama*, the conquered people, and also |*Haukhoi*, the strange people, or foreigners—*i.e.*, people of another nation or tribe. The very fact that the word Da-ma is a derivative, while Khoikhoi and Sā are not, shows us that the word Sā and Khoikhoi were formed some considerable time before Dama—that is, before the time the Khoikhoi came in contact with black races. For instance, all the names of the Khoikhoi tribes are derivatives, as can be seen from the following enumeration |Ko-bi-si, ‡Au-ni, ‡Nu-be, |Ko-ra, |Go-na, |Go-ra-χa, ||Ha-bo-be, |Ga-mi-‡nu, Ou-te-ni-, &c. This indicates that these tribes came into existence only after the agglutinative character of the Khoikhoi language was fully established, and perhaps most of them after the primitive

Khoikhoi family had separated. Here I may add that the Khoikhoi name for Betyuana is Bri or Biri (Briqua of the Cape Records), and this appellation is generally derived from *biri, goat;* thus the Tyuana are the *Goat people.* But I am more inclined to derive the word *Biri*qua from ba-*Beri,* or ba-Pedi, or ba-Beli, a Tyuana tribe, who formerly lived more to the South, in the present Free State, and are of Suto (Basuto) extraction, who form again a sub-family of the Tyuana.

Before the Khoikhoi left their primordial "Fatherland," the various degrees of relationship were already established. Father as genitor was ǁ*gŭ-b;* as protector *i-b;* as master *saub;* as friend *āb, tatab, abob* and *abo-ib.* Amongst many other names for mother was that suggestive expression *ei-gos,* the one *who looks upon*—viz., the child (from *ei* upon, and *go* to look, to see). Strange enough, uncle and grandfather, or ancestor, were called ǀǀnaub; the son-in-law was ǁnu-ri-b, and he had to spend his first years like Jacob in the service of his father-in-law. He was the *old man's* companion in the hunting-field as well as in the war. Polygamy was customary, as we can see from the appellations *gei-ris,* the *elder wife,* the *great-wife,* and ǀ*ā-ri-s,* the *younger wife.* As we shall see in the following chapter, Heitsi-eibib, their great-grandfather, had a second wife. And the laws of *succession* and *inheritance* are now-a-days the same among the surviving tribes as they were before their separation. Law, ǂhanub means what is right, straight, what is in a straight line. A *great-man's,* or, to speak more familiarly, a gentleman's, word was a *true word (amab),* and it was a disgrace to a "*great-man*" to speak untruth, or to ǂ*humi or gāra.* Boys when they became of age were told *not to lie,* not to steal ǀã, and not to ill-treat the other sex, not to commit rape. The vendetta, ǁ*kharab,* was in practice, which means *the-doing-in-return.* Sin, guilt, and wickedness was expressed by the word ǁo-re-b, evidently derived from the word ǁō, to die; ǁoreb thus means what makes *liable to death,* and ǁoreχa wicked, sinful.

All the Khoikhoi tribes use the expression *Taras* for woman. We have still the name of *Tradouw*—*i.e.*, *Tara-daob*—for a mountain-pass not far from Swellendam. *Taras* is the woman, as ruler of the house, the mistress; it is exactly the Middle-High-German *vrouwe*. The root *da* or *ta* means to conquer, to rule, to master, and the suffix *ra* expresses a custom or an intrinsic peculiarity. *Taras* is also a woman of rank, *a lady*. In every Khoikhoi's house the woman, or *taras*, is the *supreme ruler;* the husband has nothing at all to say. While in public the men take the prominent part, at home they have not so much power even as to take a mouthful of sour milk out of the tub, without the wife's permission. If a man ever should try to do it, his nearest female relations will put a fine on him, consisting in cows and sheep, which is to be added to the stock of the wife. In the house the wife always occupies the right side of the husband and the right side of the house.

If a chief died, it often happened that his energetic wife became the gau-tās (contracted from gautaras), the ruling woman—*i.e.*, the queen of the tribe—in place of the son who was not of age. Thus, the name of an old queen, Xam|hās, who ruled the Cauquas (|Khauas) at the time of Simon van der Stell, in the present Worcester district, in the valleys of the Breede river, has been handed down to us, and her descendants now live on the outskirts of the Kalihari, where they still rule the tribe, who left the Colony seventy years ago. I mean the Xam|ha, or so-called Amraal-family, ruling the Gei-|Khauas of Gobabis. Here I must mention a peculiar old custom common to all Khoikhoi tribes, and which proves how well the conjugal ties were already established before the Khoikhoi separation. ⁸All the daughters are called after the father and all the sons after the mother. Thus, if the father is Xam|*ha-b* and the mother is ‡*Arises*, the sons are—

1. ‡Ariseb geib—*i.e.*, ‡Arise the big one, or the eldest ‡Arise.

2. ‡Ariseb ‡khami, ‡Arise the younger one.

If there are three sons, then the following appellative or cognominal distinctions are made:
1. ‡Ariseb geib.
2. ‡Ariseb |naga-māb—*i.e.*, ‡Arise the-lower-standing, *i.e.*, the second.
3. ‡Ariseb ‡khami. ‡Ariseb the younger one or the youngest.

If there are four sons, the denomination runs thus:
1. ‡Ariseb geib.
2. ‡Ariseb |naga-māb.
3. ‡Ariseb ‡khami.
4. ‡Ariseb |nagā-mā-‡khami.

If there are five sons, the denomination is like the preceding, where there are four; the fifth one is called |gaob, and if it is a daughter |gaos, which means the "cut off." And if there are more than five sons, mere cognomina such as ‡nūb, the dark one, |haib, the fawn-coloured one, |awab, the red one, |nubub, the short one, ga𝜒ub, the tall one, &c., are used.

In exactly the same way the daughters are called after the father; for instance, Xam-|hab being the father, the suffix *s* of the feminine gender is simply put in place of the masculine *b* and we thus receive:—1. Xam-|hās geis. 2. Xam |has |naga-mās. 3. Xam |has ‡khams, &c. This custom will guide us, when in the sequel we have to explain the relationship of mythological persons. There is, for instance, |Urisib, the son of Heitsi-eibib. Our old storyteller did not give us the name of the wife of |Uris*ib*. But from knowing her son's name to be |Urisib, we quite correctly infer that her name certainly was |Urisi-*s*.

The eldest daughter was highly respected; to her was entirely left the milking of the cows. This was in accordance with the respect shown to the female sex in general. There is a nice charming little song illustrating this.

Ti χamse! My lioness!
!Gaibista ǀaote? Art thou afraid that I will bewitch thee?
Gomasa ke ǀausi ǁgani !omsaï!
Thou milkest the cow with a fleshy hand—*i.e.,* with a soft hand.
Natere! Bite me—*i.e.,* kiss me!
ǀGabi-ǀkhatere! Pour for me (milk)!
Ti χamse! My lioness.
Gei khoits ōase! Great man's daughter.

The uncle always calls his niece, the brother's or sister's daughter, "*Ti χamse*," my lioness.

The highest oath a man could take and still takes, was to swear by his eldest sister, and if he should abuse this name, the sister will walk into his flock and take his finest cows and sheep, and no law could prevent her from doing so. A man never can address his own sister personally; he must speak to another person to address the sister in his name, or in absence of anybody, he says so that his sister can hear, "I wish that somebody will tell my sister that I wish to have a drink of milk," &c., &c. The eldest sister can inflict even punishment on a grown-up brother, if he omits the established traditional rules of courtesy and the code of etiquette.

The art of making mats (ǀgaru-ti) and of bending poles (ǁhana-gu) for their beehive-shaped mathouses was common to all Khoikhoi; and pottery, and the manufacture of milk vessels (ǁhoe-ti), and wooden dishes (ǀoreti), and wooden basins and bowls (a-χu-ti or ǀgabi-ti), must also have been established before their pre-historic migration took place, for the substance of which their pots are made is the same, clay and ground-quartz. I have fragments of pots dug from the shores of the Southern Cape Colony, and from the outskirts of the Kalihari, which in shape and substance show no difference; and the Namaquas of the present day still make pots in the old style, though traders sell to them iron pots very cheap (pot sū-s, to boil, to cook sāi). Food, especially meat, is always well boiled, and not underdone, as our gourmands prefer it.

We must also conclude that the process of melting ore was known to the Khoikhoi before their general separation; for |urib is the word for *iron* or any other metal used by all clans and tribes, and is derived from |ū, to separate (intransitive and transitive), German *ausscheiden*. They also manufactured knives, spears (gōagu), and metal rings both of copper and iron, as ornaments for arms and legs. (Rings |ganugu, literally meaning the ties, from |gai to bind.) From the invention of iron tools, such as knives and axes and spears, it was only a short step to the fabrication (||hoe-χoa-!na) of wooden vessels in which they could keep their milk and fat.

But iron and copper tools were, on account of the difficulty of manufacturing them, as yet too valuable; consequently the stone implements of the more primitive age were not entirely abandoned. That a Stone Age must have existed among the Hottentots is proved by the fact that the priest (!gai-aob) up to this day never uses an iron knife, but always a splint of a sharp quartz, when he has to perform the rite of making a boy a man, or if he has to make an operation, or if a sheep or cow is slaughtered as an offering to the deceased or to the Supreme Being.

Oxen were broken in for the purpose of carrying and riding (!gabi), and men and women both were experts in the art of riding, much unlike the Kafir, who will ride while his wife and children have to trot alongside of him. Van Riebeeke's journal in the Cape Archives of 1658 speaks of *pack-oxen;* and also Vasco da Gama, when he came to Mosselbay, saw * women riding on oxen down to the Bay to see the *new comer* (the ship of da Gama).

It speaks well for the refined taste of the ancient Khoikhoi, that they were fond of perfumes (sā-b or buχu).

---

* "Their brides on slow-paced oxen ride behind."—CAMOENS, *The Lusiad.* Book V.

The most costly present lovers could lavish on each other was buχu, and these sweet aromatic herbs of a certain Diosma were also sprinkled on those cairns which still are objects of worship, and where they assembled to offer prayers to the deceased or to the Supreme Being Tsũi‖goab. We know that in the earliest times a large trade was carried on (‖amab, trade, ‖amagu, to trade, to exchange, to barter), not only with pottery, dishes, spears, and knives, but chiefly with Buχu. And the leaves of the *Diosma* growing on the Khamies Bergen, the Lange Zwarte Bergen (‡Nu-‖khara, a name still remembered by the old men of the ǀAmas tribe), and of the ǀKhomab Mountains in Great Namaqualand, and of ‡Nu-ǃhoas opposite Sandwich harbour, were known all over the Khoikhoi territory.

That the eyes of the ancient Khoikhoi were early directed towards the sky, we shall see from a myth in the following chapter. The stars too were an early object of contemplation to them, as is evident from the number of names for the stars. Certain it is that the ǀ*Khãseti* (ǀKhunuseti) or Pleiades, the Belt of Orion or ǀ*goregu* the Zebras, *a* Orionis χ*ami*, the Lion, *a* Tauri (Aldebaran) *aob*, the husband, were known to all the Khoikhoi before the separation. There was a star-mythology, and things in the blue vault went on in the same way as here on earth.

The ancient Khoikhoi were a brave and warlike people, and it characterizes their wars that women and children were spared. *War* was *torob*, from *toro*, to *bore*, to *perforate*; thus war means the perforator. Bravery was highly admired, and girls used to meet the victorious heroes (ǃgari-b, ‖gob, ǃë-aob) who returned to the kraals laden with booty, singing their praise. Such heroes had then to undergo a ceremony. The priest or ǃgaiaob cut certain marks on the chest of the brave man with a flint stone, and he received then on such an occasion a cognomen as Xama-ǃgamteb, Lion-killer, ‖Otsãtamab, The One who cannot die, Aogu‖ōb, Destroyer of heroes, &c. Names of places and rivers up to this day tell us of battles once fought, such as |Khami and |Khams, Battlefield, |Kho-||oa-tes, " You cannot catch me ;" |Khotoas, the last one caught ; ‡Kχiχas, peace ; |Huritamas, " I am not afraid." Other names again bear testimony to the love for dancing and singing, like |Gaĩ||nais and |Gaĩ||naiχas, " Good, pleasant singing," ‡Aχaĩs, "Reed-dance." And even sentimental feelings seem to be as characteristic of them as of the writers of fashionable novels now-a-days. ||Â||ōs, " Dying from love," has probably been the scene of a very tragical love affair.

Prophets (gebo-aogu, *i.e.*, seers) could tell to new-born children as well as to heroes their fate, and this important institution was in the hands of the greatest and most respected old men of the clan. We shall see hereafter that Heitsieibib, Tsu-||goab and the Moon, all were endowed with the power of prophecy.

I have already shown in the forms derived from *khoi*, that the Khoikhoi are able to form abstract words.

This distinguishes them most favourably from all the Bushmen tribes, and proves how high their mental development must have been before they emigrated from their primitive territory.

I shall give only a few specimens. ‡*Eĩ*, to think, from ‡*ani* to cut to pieces, to slaughter, hence, ‡*eĩs* (‡*anis*), the thought ; ‡*eĩ*-‡*eĩ-sen*, to consider, to think over again ; ‡*eĩ*-‡*eĩ-sen-s*, the result of one's own consideration, idea, perception.

Î, to appear, to shine ; *ĩsib*, form, shape, likeness, appearance ; *ĩsa* and *iχa*, full of form, beautiful, pretty, handsome.

Sĩ, to come, to arrive ; *sĩ* (from sini), to cause to arrive— *i.e.*, to send ; *sĩsen*, to send oneself—*i.e.*, *to work ;* German, *sich anschicken.*

A, yes ; *ama*, true ; amab, truth ; amasib, truthfulness, love of truth.

|Nams, love, fondness ; nam|namsa, fond, dear ; |nam, to love.

|Amo, eternal, endless, |amosib, eternity. This |amo is derived from |ā to be sharp, to be pointed; hence |amo, the end, the point; *o* is used as the *a privativum* in Greek, and means without. Thus |amo, what is without end.

|Khom, to have mercy; |khoms, mercy.

|u, to forget; |ũ, to forgive—*i.e.*, to forget the hatred.

‡Khā, to refuse; ‡khaba, stubborn, wicked; ‡*khabasib*, wickedness, badness. Why missionaries have committed the absurdity of forming from a Hebrew root the word *elo*χ*oresa*—*i.e.*, being without élohim—is to me a riddle, when we have a very pregnant Khoikhoi word to express wicked and wickedness.

Tsã, to feel; *tsãb*, the feeling, taste, sentiment; *tsã|kha*, to feel with—*i.e.*, to condole; tsâ-|khasib, condolence (German Mitgefühl).

|*Anu*, clean, neat; but *anu*, sacred, pure, refined, handsome, beautiful; also *anu*χ*a* ; anusib, holiness, sacredness, purity.

To show what the Khoikhoi mean by *anu* and *anu*χ*a*, I may give the following conversation I once had with an old Namaqua. A girl, a niece of his, used to bring daily some milk to my camp. Her lovely face and the pure expression of the eyes had struck me repeatedly, and I could not help being complimentary to the old man. It was indeed one of those faces

> "Which tell of days in goodness spent,
> A mind in peace with all below,
> A heart whose love is innocent."

I used in my conversation the word īsa (beautiful), when the old man almost indignantly said, "No, every girl can be īsa, but such an appearance as hers we call *anu*χ*a* (full of purity)." This was amongst Khoikhoi who had no missionary yet, and who still lived in national primitive independence.

Nothing, however, is more convincing of the abstract power of the Khoikhoi language than the great number

of names for the various divisions and subdivisions of
colours. The colour itself is *îsib*—*i.e.*, appearance. It
must be remembered that the colours named in the following are not all which are known to the Khoikhoi,
which must surprise the more if we recollect that they
have been collected in the most barren territory of South
Africa, in Great Namaqualand. For this reason we need
not doubt that, among the other tribes, not only the same
words were in existence, but that also more subdivisions
were known. Be this however as it may, we are
told that Demokritus knew only of four colours, and that
in China the number of colours was originally five, while
we shall learn from the following that the Khoikhoi distinguished very strictly between [1]|uri, white, [2] ǂnū, black,
[3]!am, green, [4]|awa (|aua, |ava), red, [5]ǂhoa, blue, [6]|hai,
fawn-coloured, [7]|huni, yellow, [8]ǂgama, brown, [9]|khau,
grey, [10]|naiǂu, [11]|garu, dotted. Then we have the following subdivisions—[1]|uri-|huni, whitish-yellow, [2]|urisi,
whitish, [3]ǂnu-|ho, black-patched, [4]ǂnu-|garu, black-dotted, [5]ǂnu-ǂura, black-shining (German, *schwarz-schillernd*), [6]|ava-ǂura, red-shining, [7]|ava-ǂgani, with white
and red patches, [8]|awa-|ho or |gi-|ho, chestnut-colour,
[9]|avara or |avaχa, reddish, [10]|am-ǂura, green-shining (for
instance, the colour of the Naja Haje); [11]ǂgama-|ho, brown-dotted, [12]ǂgama-|garu, the same, [13]ǂgama-ǂhoa, brownish-blue (the colour of Bucephalus Capensis); [14]ǂgama-ǂura,
brown-shining, like the Vipera Cornuta. The colour of
the rainbow is always |am, green; only in two cases I
heard that it was considered to be |ava, red. The name
of the rainbow is tsawirub and dabitsirub. In Bible
translations of missionaries we read |avi-|hanab. This
is very incorrect, and nothing else but a verbal translation of *rain-bow*. As to tsawirub, the etymology is not
quite clear; tsawib is the ebony-tree, which much resembles in appearance the weeping willow; the leaves are
dark green, ǂnu-|am, and *tsaba*χ*a* bile-coloured, from
tsabab, the bile. Now it is difficult to say whether the

ebony-tree has been called after the green colour of the bile, and also whether the rainbow, *tsawirub*, received its name from *tsabab*. ǃUri is a derivative from the original ǃū, and certainly has with ǀubus, egg, the root ǃu in common; consequently ǃuri means egg-coloured, and the egg *par excellence*, the ostrich egg, is white. The same root for white and egg we had in the ǀAi Bushman language. ǀAm, green, means originally *springing up*, or *shooting forth*, like in German *ausschlagend*, used for the fresh green leaves; ǀa, to hit, ǂnou-ǀa, and ǂnou-ǀan, to beat —to hit, German, *treffen*; ǁnau-ǀa and ǁnau-ǀan to hear —to hit, *i.e.*, to understand; mũ-ǀa and mũ-ǀan, to see or to look—to hit, *i.e.*, to observe, to perceive, to acknowledge. ǀAva, red, is nothing else but ǀaua, blood-coloured, from ǀau, to bleed, or ǀau-b, blood. ǃHuni is yellow, that is, the colour of clay or ground, from ǃhu-b, ground, earth, clay. ǂGama, brown, is the colour of ǂgāb, originally ǂgamab, the colour of a *vley*; the vley is a water-pond, which is dry in the winter, and then the bottom shows a brown colour. ǀKhan, grey, is the colour of the ǀkhani, Bos elaphus. ǀNai-ǂu is the colour of the ǃnaib, giraffe and also of the zebra. ǀGaru is dotted like a leopard, hence this animal is called ǀgarub. The other name of ǀgarub, leopard, however, is more significant; he is also called χoasaūb, the mark— scratcher, from χoa to scratch, and saū to mark, to imprint.

I cannot conclude this chapter without adding some remarks on Khoikhoi poetry, and on the so-called "*Reed-dance*," ǂāb, to which in the following chapters repeatedly reference will be made.

The Khoikhoi have two kinds of poetry, sacred and profane. The sacred hymns, as well as the profane songs, are sung accompanied by the so-called Reed-music or Reed-dancers. The sacred hymns are generally prayers, invocations, and songs of praise in honour of Tsuǁgoab, Heitsieibib, and the Moon; and such sacred songs, and the performance with dancing is called ǀgeib while the general profane songs are called ǁnai-tsanati, and to perform them with a dance on reed-pipes, or better, barkpipes, is ǂaba χaïre. The profane reed-dances or reedsongs are of a very different nature. Either the fate of a hero who fell in a battle or lost his life on a hunting expedition, is deplored; and on such an occasion a performance is connected with it. In such a case the performances have much in common with the mediæval German "Singspiel." We can also compare them with our modern operas. If an illustrious stranger visits a place, he is often welcomed with a reed-dance while entering the place. Thus the first Moravian missionary, George Schmidt, who came to the ǁHeisiqua Hottentots in the Calodon district, was received with a reed-dance. The Dutch Governor van der Stell, on his journey to the Copper Mountains, the present Copper mines, was honoured in the same way. Hop, a burgher of Stellenbosch, who in Governor Ryk van Tulbagh's time went on an expedition to Great Namaqualand, received the congratulations of the ǁHabobes at the foot of the ǁKharas mountain in a grand reed-dance performance. Alexander received the same honours from his Namaqua host, the famous Jonker Afrikaner ǀHaramūb; and up to this time the traveller, if he only understand how to fraternize with them, will gladly be admitted to witness their simple merry-making.

If chiefs have become unpopular by some whimsical or despotic orders, very soon the tongue of the women—of whom a Khoikhoi proverb says "that they cannot be as long quiet as it takes sweet milk to get sour"—will lecture him in a sarcastic reed-song. Once I saw a chief sitting by, when the young girls sung into his face, telling him "that he was a hungry hyena and a roguish jackal; that he was the brown vulture who is not only satisfied with tearing the flesh from the bones, but also feasted on the intestines." On another occasion, a very old man had married a very young girl, and her friends sung:

The geiris (first wife) is dismissed, his only great thought is the ǀaris (second wife); or, as we should say, "Age does not prevent a man making a fool of himself."

Other songs again are of a very simple character: "Don't, please, kill my antelope, my darling antelope; my antelope is so poor; my antelope is an orphan,"—and are simply an instance of the thrift of poetical productiveness. Or they are of a comical nature, sympathizing with a patient who suffers from gripes:

Poor young ǁKharis got into a fright,
She is suffering from gripes,
And bites the ground like the hyena which ate poison.
The people run to see the fun!
They all were very much frightened!
And still they say—oh, it is nothing!

This reminds one very much of the style of Heinrich Heine; and even more of the way of the Middle-High-German poet, Nithart. I saw this play, "The Gripes," performed, and honestly confess that I laughed until the tears came. Helmerding could here have found his match in caricaturing people.

Every larger kraal has its bandmaster, *ei-ǃgun-aob*, the leader. He teaches the young boys how to perform and to play on the pipes, and if a boy should remain out of class, he is sure to get the whip severely. Also the girls, if they are too lazy and do not pay attention enough, receive now and then the whip, but then generally on the kaross, merely to make a noise and to frighten them. The reed-music sounds exactly like the playing on a harmonium. It is very pleasant indeed to hear it at a distance. Boys who perform well, are petted by the girls, and this kind of petting is called ǀ*kho-*ǀ*kha*, *to touch the body*, which means, "to praise a person in a song."

Such was the culture of the Khoikhoi before they migrated from the grave of ǀGurikhoisib, and such was it still at the time when Bartolomeo Diaz discovered the Cape, and when Governor Jan van Riebeeke hoisted the banner of the Netherlands at the foot of Table Mountain, below the old Khoikhoi kraal ⁹||Hu-!gais. And such we find it still to be amongst the tribes of Great Namaqualand, and the remnants of the |Kora and the so-called Cape Hottentots.

The orthography of the few specimens of the old Khoikhoi language of the Cape Colony, given by Witsen, Kolb, Valentyn, Ludolf, Leibniz, Thunberg, Spaarman, Le Vaillant, Barrow, Liechtenstein, Burchell, &c., is very much distorted, when compared with that of the excellent publications of Schmelen, Knudsen, Vollmer, and Tindall. Nevertheless, the language of the Khoikhoi tribes, such as the Kochoquas, Charigurunas, Hessaquas, Outeniquas, Attaquas, now swept from the face of the earth, and the present living idioms of the Namaquas, !Gonaquas, |Khauas, !Amas, and !Koras, and few remnants of the Chrichriquas, the present Griquas, show the same structure, the same sex-denoting tendency, the same agglutinative peculiarity, the same decimal system of counting, and an equal abundance of abstract ideas and expressions well fitted to interpret the most sublime and sacred feelings of the human heart.

An unmerciful fate has overtaken the Khoikhoi; the most powerful tribes have been annihilated, and with them their traditions, sacred as well as profane. Those still extant have lost so much of their national peculiarities by contact with civilization, and have adopted such a number of Indo-European beliefs and customs; and the Christian ideas introduced by missionaries have amalgamated to such a degree with the national religious ideas and mythologies, that for this reason I have in the following pages preferred to give less than I could give, lest I should be accused that from a certain natural interest in, and sympathy with, the Khoikhoi, I had been carried away to assign to them a higher station in the scale of culture than they are entitled to claim. I wanted to represent the religious ideas of the Khoikhoi and the worship of their Supreme Being in its true light, and had therefore to leave out every legend or myth, which, although it may be genuine, gives to the foreigner reason to believe that it savours too much of missionary influence.

A friend of mine the other day in Cape Town, when we were speaking about the traditions of the South African races, told me in a blunt way that these stories were insipid, and some even very repulsive; no sensible and educated man would look at them! I had to remind my friend that, as to the repulsiveness, he simply showed that he was very little acquainted with Greek mythology, and as to the charge of being insipid, the same was said at the beginning of the Nursery Tales collected by Grimm, which are now translated into Dutch and English; and that men of world-wide experience are happy to fill up their leisure hours with reading those simple tales over again, which, in their childhood, were heard from the lips of some old nurse.

To the man of science, these so-called insipid and repulsive stories have the same interest as the Bathybius Haeckelii has to the biologist, and a common lichen to the botanist, who would perhaps pass unnoticed a famous race-horse, or a gigantic cabbage.

NOTES TO THE FIRST CHAPTER.

[1] Tsûi-ǁgoab, &c. On the title-page I have written Tsuni-ǁgoam, because this is the reconstructed original form. The nasal ˜ was originally an *n* or *m;* thus we have still the forms ǀhu*n*-khoib and ǀhũ-khoib, ‡*Anisa*-‡gaobeb and ‡*Aīsa*-‡gaobeb, ‡*Gama*-‡gorib and ‡Gã-‡gorib, ǀ*Khuni* and ǀ*Khũi*, &c. As to the suffix *m* in ǁgoa*m*, it is more primitive than *b*. Some Cape Dialects, and especially the ǀKora, have preserved *m*

where the Nama uses *b*; thus, ǀKora ǁkhām, Nama ǁkhāb; ǀKora ǀgām, Nama ǀgāb; ǀKora mūm, Nama mūb, &c. &c. *Vide* Th. Hahn, "Die Sprache der Nama" (Leipzig, 1870), p. 67, 3; also p. 29, sub Dritte Person, and p. 65, ‡gā.

[2] As to the prehistoric condition of the Hottentot race, *vide* Th. Hahn, "The Graves of Heitsi-eibib," in the *Cape Monthly Magazine* (May, 1878), and Friedr. Müller, "Allgemeine Ethnographie" (Wien, 1879), pp. 78 and 93, &c.

[3] Cattle, sheep, and goats. All the records of the Dutch and English and Portuguese navigators agree on the point that the Khoikhoi they met with at St. Helena Bay, Saldanha Bay, the Cape, Mossel Bay, Algoa Bay, were rich in cattle and sheep. The Hottentot sheep is particularly known for its long tail and hair in place of wool. We are led to believe that the Central African natives originally had no sheep. Certainly the Kafir, the Zulu, the Tyuana, the Herero (Damara), and Mbò had no sheep; and the present Herero sheep is the true type of the old Hottentot sheep. The Herero come from the heart of Africa, from parts where no sheep are to be met with.

[4] Of the hospitality and kind-heartedness of the Khoikhoi, Kolb and Valentyn give some striking proofs. It is also a prominent feature in the character of the Khoikhoi that they are *not* inclined to steal.

[5] In the "Idioticon Hamburgense," p. 101, by Michael Richey (Hamburg, 1755), there is the following remark:— "Hüttentüth, Schimpfwort auf einen unnützen Artzt, welcher beim gemeinen Mann heisset: Doctor Hüttentüth, de den Lüden dat water besüht." Then again, "Bremisch Niedersächsisch Wörterbuch" (ii. p. 678):—" Hüttentüt, so nennt der gemeine Mann in Hamburg einen Stümper in der Arzney Kunst." Both remarks evidently show that the word Hütentüt, or Hottentot, means something irregular, something which is out of order, something

extraordinary and confused. Dapper, in his excellent work, " Umbständliche und Eigentliche Beschreibung von Africa" (Amsterdam, 1670), p. 626, expressly says that the name Hottentot has been given by the Dutch to the natives they found at the Cape of Good Hope, on account of the curious clicks and harsh sounds in that language, and "that the Dutch also apply as a reproach the word *Hottentot* to one who stammers and stutters too much with the tongue." Sutherland, therefore, in his " Memoir respecting the Kaffers, Hottentots, and Bosjemans of South Africa" (Cape Town, 1846), ii. p. 2, footnote, in what he says about the origin of the word Hottentot is wrong. " It appears," says this author, "that the term Hottentot is either an original native appellation, belonging to some tribe farther north or north-east (which tribe is apparently lost), and applied to the inhabitants of the neighbourhood of the Cape by the early Portuguese settlers on the coast; but the meaning of the term it would seem almost impossible to trace, as hitherto its roots have not been found either in the Portuguese, the Dutch, the Hottentot, the Arabic, or the Sichuana languages, although sought for by some learned persons who have taken much interest in the research. Yet the Arabic word *oote*, to strike with a club, and again the word *toote*, a missile or projectile of any kind, referring to the well-known weapon of the Hottentot as well as of the Kaffer, may favour the idea of its Arabic origin, to which the Dutch might have added the Holland, for it is sometimes found Hollandootes.—(*Where ?*)— Hence, perhaps, the corruption Hottentootes. Hollondootes would thus mean, of course, a people struck down —conquered by Holland."

⁶ Ku-néne, means nothing else than the Great River, from the adjective néne in the Mbó language, meaning, great, big, large. The derivation of Zambesi is not quite clear, but so much we know, that this river was known by that name already to the early Portuguese. On a very old coloured map of Africa, from about the year 1600,

we find the River *Zambere*; on the map attached to Dapper's work the *Zambere* is also marked. Valentyn, in his admirable work on the Dutch East Indian Colonies, gives a map, on which also a part of South Africa is sketched, and where the said river is pretty fairly laid down with the two names *Zambesi* and *Empondo*. The Kunene's name is also to be found with the quite correct translation " Groote Rivier."

[7] *Goreb.*—That the Khoikhoi transferred other names of certain parts of the body, or utensils and furniture, to plants, is quite evident from the following examples:— ||oāb, arm and branch of a tree; ‡geigu, the ears, and the leaves of the trees and plants; ||haran, the flowers, or little pockets from ||hās or ||hōs pocket, bag. We, for instance, call a certain flower in Germany *Pantoffelblume*—i.e., the slipper-flower.

[8] *All the daughters are called after the father.*—Mr. G. Theal, our excellent South African historian and custodian of the colonial archives, who spent many years among the frontier Kafirs, N!gika and |Galeka, informs me that they have adopted the same way of name-giving from the Khoikhoi, and that this custom is still in vogue at the present day. Here we have also, as in so many other instances, an evidence that the Khoikhoi exercised an influence on the Kafir.

[9] *||Hu-|gais.*—This is the name by which Cape Town is known wherever the Khoikhoi tongue is spoken. This name consists of two words, ||hū the root of a verb, meaning " to condense," hence ||hū-s, an old word for *cloud*, the word is still used; ||hūs is also a game, and especially the game where |Gurikhoisib, who is also called ‡Eiχa|kha||nabiseb, or *lightning*, loses all his copper beads. This is metaphor; and ||hūs or the ||hūs game is the game, battle, or fight in the clouds—the thunderstorm. In the thunderstorm ‡Eiχa|kha||nabiseb loses the lightning, which falls down to the earth; |gai is to bind, to surround, to tie, to envelop. ||Hu-|gais

consequently means " veiled in clouds." And, indeed, every inhabitant of Cape Town will admit that this is a very significant name for "Table-mountain." We still say, if the clouds envelop the top of "Table-mountain," he has his "tablecloth" on.

CHAPTER II.

The religious instinct should be honoured even in dark and confused mysteries.—SCHELLING.

SACRED FRAGMENTS AND RELICS.

IN this chapter I propose to give extracts from the accounts of former travellers as much as my own observations, reserving for my next chapter the inferences I have drawn from them.

Worship of Heitsi-eibib.

Corporal Müller, travelling with the Hottentot interpreter Harry along the False Bay, east of the Cape, in October, 1655, says:

"We were marching generally in a S.E. direction; after marching half an hour one morning we saw a strange proceeding of the Hottentot women on the side of our path, where a *great stone* lay. Each woman had a *green* branch in her hand, laid down upon her face on the stone, and spoke words, which we did not understand; on asking what it meant, they said, 'Hette hie,' and pointed above, as if they would say, 'It is an offering to God.'"—("Sutherland Memoir respecting the Kaffers, Hottentots, and Bosjesmans," vol. ii. p. 88.)

As will be seen from the sequel of this chapter, the word "*Hette hie*" is only a distortion of "*Heitsi-eibib*," and the form of worship, described here at the cairn, is nothing else but the Heitsi-eibib worship, as it is practised still up to this day all over Great Namaqualand and in

!Koranaland, where Heitsi-eibib has changed names, and the worship is offered to |Garubeb or Tsũi-||goab.

Worship of Tsũi-||goab (Dawn), ||Khab (Moon) and Heitsi-eibib (Dawn-tree).

Dapper, as early as 1671, speaking of the Khoikhoi at the Cape of Good Hope, says:

"They know and believe that there is *One*, whom they call *humma* or *summa* (*i.e.*, in Nama or |Kora |*homi, heaven*), who sends rain on earth, who makes the winds blow, and who makes the heat and the cold. . . . .

"They also believe that they themselves can make rain, and can prevent the wind from blowing. . . . .

"It appears also that there is a certain superstition about the new moon. For if the moon is seen again (the new moon) they crowd together, making merry the whole night, dancing, jumping, and singing; clasping their hands together, and also murmuring some words (singing hymns). . . . .

"Nay, their women and children are seen to kneel before erected stones and bow before them."—(O. Dapper, "Umbständliche und Eigentliche Beschreibung von Africa." Amsterdam, 1671, pp. 626, 627.)

Heitsi-eibib, or Tsũi-||goab, Worship.

Nicolas Witsen, burgomaster of Amsterdam, communicates to his learned friend Jobst Ludolf, in Germany, the following interesting letter, dated Cape of Good Hope, February 19, 1691, forty years after the landing of Governor Jan van Riebeeke at the Cape:

"Nobilissimus vir miscebat sermonem cum aliquot Hottentottis, qui pro sua erga ipsum familiaritate docebant nihil dissimulando [1] '*se adorare Deum certum aliquem*' cuius caput manus seu pugni magnitudinem haberet; grandi eundem esse et deducto in latitudinem corpore; auxilium vero eius implorari tempore famis et anonae carioris aut alterius cuiuscunque necessitatis. Uxores suas solere caput Dei conspergere terra rubra, (torob) Buchu et aliis suave olentibus herbis, oblato quoque eidem sacrificio non uno. Ex quo demum intelligi coeptum est, Hottentottos colere etiam aliquem [2] Deum!

Tsūi-||goab, |Guru-b, and ||Gaunab.

Valentyn, a very trustworthy authority, who was a man of high education and of a classical training, and who had an eye to observe what many others overlooked, tells us in the fifth volume of his great work "Keurlyke Beschryving van Choromandel, &c. &c., vol. v. p. 109 : "I heard from the chieftains and various others that they call ' *God*' in their language not only the '*Great Chief*,' in saying, if it thunders, the *Great Chief* is angry with us; but they generally call ' God' in their language *Thukwa* or *Thik-qua* (Tsūi-||goab); but the *Supreme Ruler* they call *Khourrou*; the *Devil, Dangoh* and *Damoh*; a *Spectre* whom they fear very much, *somsoma*." And p. 158 our author continues: "I must say, that I really observed many things amongst them which looked like religious worship. . . . .

"It is certain, when the new moon reappears, they have that whole night a great merry-making and clasping of hands. They also, ten or twelve of them, sit on the banks of a river together, and throw some balls or dumplings, made of clay, into the water. . . . . It also is certain that I often heard them speaking of a *Great Chief* who dwells on high, whom they call in their own language *Thikwa* or *Thukwa*, and to whom they showed respect, especially during great storms of thunder and lightning. They also know of a *Devil*, whom they call *Damoh*, a black chief, who does much harm to them; they avoided speaking of him, as he often persecuted them; but in carefully examining this, it is nothing else but their *somsomas* and *spectres*. Some of them also call the Supreme, *Lord* (Nama |Khūb) from which it is evident that they believe in more than one [3] *Khourrou*."

'Valentyn then continues telling us that he had a conversation with a Hottentot who had been trained by the Dutch clergyman van Kalden, and he (Valentyn) found the man so well informed about the Christian religion and discovered in him such an understanding of religious matters that it was quite a pleasure to hear him speaking. As to Valentyn, he touched on his return voyage from the East Indies, in 1705, at the Cape. He ha(been a minister of the gospel in Amboina, &c., for mor than twenty years, and took a great interest in native customs and manners, of which he had acquired a great knowledge.

||*Khāb, the Moon, and* |*Khūb, the Lord.*

The missionaries Plütschau and Ziegenbalg, sent by the King of Denmark, Frederic IV. to India in the commencement of the eighteenth century, touched at the Cape, where they had an opportunity of intercourse with the Hottentots (Khoikhoi).

Plütschau saw how the natives danced in the moonlight, singing and clasping their hands together. The missionary asked whether they worshipped the Moon? The answer was, that they could not exactly say this, but it was the old custom of their ancestors to do so. *They worshipped a Great Chief.*—(W. Germann, Ziegenbalg und Plütschau, Erlangen, 1868, pp. 62.)

||*Khāb, the Moon, and* |*Khūb, the Lord.*

Another traveller of the seventeenth century, Wilhelm Vogel, tells us about the Khoikhoi he met at the Cape: " Of God and His nature they know very little or nothing, although one can observe that they have some worship of the moon. At new moon they come together and make a noise the whole night, dancing in a circle, and while dancing they clasp their hands together. Sometimes they are seen in dark caves, where they offer some prayers, which, however, a European does not understand. While doing this they have a very curious behaviour, they turn their eyes towards the sky and one makes to the other a cross on the forehead. And this is, perhaps, a kind of religious worship."—(Wilhelm Vogel, " Ostindianische Reise," p. 67.)

||Khāb, the Moon ; Tsūi-||goab, the Dawn ; |Khūb, the Lord ; ||Gaunab, the Destroyer.

We now come to the worthy German Magister, Peter Kolb, whose reports have been repeatedly doubted by European writers, but without any good reason. Any traveller or missionary who is well acquainted with the manners and customs of the Bergdamaras, a black tribe in Great Namaqualand, which entirely has adopted Namaqua manners and language, and which preserved these elements even much better than the Namaquas themselves, will endorse the greater part of Kolb's book on the Hottentots. The good and kind-hearted old Magister bore no hatred against the natives, and he is a great admirer of their simple and unvarnished manners. He has paid special attention to the religion and worship of these savages, and his observations on this subject deserve well to be noticed. Kolb quotes first from other authors, and gives last, but not least, his own observations :—

" Saar, an officer of the Dutch Government (p. 157), distinctly says : ' One does not know what kind of religion they have, but early, *when the day dawns*, they assemble and take each other by the hands and dance, and call out in their language towards the heavens. From this one may conclude that they must have some idea of the Godhead.' "—(Peter Kolb, p. 406. German edition. Nüremberg, 1719.)

From Father Tachard, Kolb also quotes : " These people know nothing of the creation of the world .... nothing of the Trinity in the Godhead .... *but they pray to a God.*"—(Kolb, p. 406.)

The contemporary of Kolb and Ziegenbalg, was also a Danish missionary, Böving, who says : " *There are some rudera and traces of an idea (perception) of a God. For they know, at least the more intelligent among them, that there is a God*, who has made the earth and heavens, who causes thunder and rain, and who gives them food and skins for clothing, so that also of them may be said what St. Paul says, Rom. i. 19."—(Kolb, p. 406.)

Kolb's own experience runs thus: "It is obvious that all Hottentots believe in a God, they know him and confess it; to him they ascribe the work of creation, and they maintain that he still rules over everything and that he gives life to everything. On the whole he is possessed of such high qualities that they could not well describe him. . . . . Then our author continues, that nobody has given better information on the subject than the above-mentioned Böving.

"Because the station of a chief is the highest charge, therefore they call the Lord *⁶ Gounia*, and they call the moon so, as their visible God. But if they mean the Invisible, and intend to give him his true name, they call him Gounia Tiquaa—*i.e.*, the God of all gods. He is *a good man and does not do any harm to them*, and therefore they need not be afraid of him?" Kolb affirms that his own experience, gathered during a long residence among the natives, is, "*that the Khoikhoi give the moon the name of the Great Chief.*" He had observed how they performed dances in honour of the new moon, and how they address the moon in singing: "Be welcome, give us plenty of honey, give grass to our cattle, that we may get plenty of milk." In offering this prayer they look towards the moon.

After our author has described the whole performances, and all the rites connected with the religious worship of the Hottentots, he exclaims: "And who now dares to deny that this dancing, singing, and offering invocations at the time of the full moon and new moon, is not a religious worship?" (P. 412.)

I need not quote any more authorities on this subject.

It may suffice to state, that I have observed the same dancing and singing towards the moon, and that I fully can endorse Kolb's statements. As will be seen in another page of this essay, the moon really is considered to be a deity, *who promises men immortality.*

But to return to our worthy Magister, he speaks also of another being, whom he calls the *other Captain of less power*, from whom some of the natives (the sorcerers, |gai-aogu) have learnt witchcraft. *He never does good to men, but always harm. They, therefore, must fear him, show respect to him, and serve him.*

This coincides, according to my own experience, with the ||Gauna worship of the ‡Auni tribe, close to Walefish Bay and Sandwich Harbour, who offer prayers to ||Gauna, although they call him an evil-doer, who even kills them when they are out hunting. If Kolb says the name of this being is *Touquoa*, then he is mistaken; he has simply misunderstood his informer.

On pages 416, 417, and 418, Kolb speaks of the worship of the Mantis insect. This has been doubted by various authorities. But from what I often had occasion to observe, Kolb's remarks are quite correct. The Namaquas believe that this insect brings luck if it creeps on a person, and one is not allowed to kill it. Strange enough, they call it also ||Gaunab, as they call the 'enemy of Tsũi-|| goab.

At the conclusion of his remarks on the religion of the Khoikhoi, Kolb supplies us with some valuable information about the places of worship. He says: "These Hottentots have neither churches nor chapels, made with the hands of men, but they consider in their mind that certain places are sacred, because their ancestors have received great luck at such spots. Those places are to be found in the deserts, and consist of stone heaps, others are rivers, ... and they never pass such a deserted spot or hill without offering worship to the saint who, according to their belief, inhabits the place, and who has done so much good to so many of them." (P. 418.)

"Once on an occasion," says Kolb, "a Hottentot ||Kamma, whom I caught in the act of dancing and singing round such a spot, told me, that he, on a journey, slept at this place, and was not devoured by a lion who approached him during the night at a few yards distance only. He, the Hottentot, could not help thinking that a saint (ghost) inhabited the spot, and had protected him, and he considered it his duty not to forget this ⁸ kindness." (P. 419.)

Tsũi-||goab, and |Khunuseti, the Pleiades.

The first Khoikhoi missionary, George Schmidt, was sent in 1737 by the Moravian Mission to the Cape. He settled amongst the Hessaquas, a tribe inhabiting the present Caledon district, on the banks of the Zondereinde River. The place formerly called Baviaanskloof, now Genadendal, is still occupied by the United Brethren.

"At the return of the Pleiades," says Schmidt, "these natives celebrate an anniversary; as soon as these stars appear above the eastern horizon mothers will lift their little ones on their arms, and running up to elevated spots, will show to them those friendly stars, and teach them to stretch their little hands towards them. The people of a kraal will assemble to dance and to sing according to the old custom of their ancestors.

"The chorus always sings: 'O Tiqua, our Father above our heads, give rain to us, that the fruits (bulbs, &c.), uientjes, may ripen, and that we may have plenty of food, send us a good year.' "—(⁹ *Basler Magazin*, 1831, p. 12, and Burkhard's "Missionsgeschichte," Africa, vol. ii. p. 9.)

Tsũi-||goab.

In the Appendix to his Travels, De Jong, commander of a Dutch vessel, who spent a considerable time at the Cape, quotes from George Schmidt's reports, and says: "They have no religion or rites, and they only believe that there is a Lord, whom they call Tui'qua. They also believe in a devil, to whom they give the name 'Gauna, but they do not care much about him."—(De Jong, "Reisen nach dem Vorgebürge der guten Hoffnung," Hamburg, 1803, vol. i. p. 274.)

||Kháb, the Moon, and |Khub, the Lord.

By order of the Dutch Governor, Ryk van Tulbagh, an expedition was undertaken to the Great Namaquas, which reached as far as the Kamob river, about lat. 27°. In the [10] Journal of Hop, the commander of that expedition, we find the following remark: "Their (the Namaqua) religion chiefly consists in worshipping and praising the new moon. The men stand in a circle together and blow on a hollow pipe or similar instrument, and the women, clasping hands, dance round the men. They continually sing in a praying manner, that the last moon had protected them and their cattle so well, and they hope the same from this new moon. The Cabonas (very likely the ||Habona or ||Haboben) whom we met, praised the moon, particularly that *he* (in Hottentot the moon is masculine) had brought them into contact with a nation from whom they had received so much kindness. Although these were the only rites, *we also observed that they had some idea of a Supreme Being, whom they call Chuyn* (the Nama |Khūb or |Khunib), and who is great and powerful. For if they want to express that something is beyond their conception, then they say it is a work of 'Chuyn."—("Hop's Journal," pp. 88, 89.)

Heitsi-eibib, ||Gaunab, and |Gurub.

We should have expected that the Swedish travellers, Thunberg and Sparrmann, men of great learning, would have been able to give us more particular information about the religion of the Khoikhoi. It, however, appears that their great learning on the one side made them underrate the natives. On the other hand, the natives, as sensitive as children to the thinly disguised contempt of the foreigners, rendered fruitless all attempts to gain deeper insight into their religious ideas, partly through a natural shyness and fear of ridicule, but chiefly through a stubborn unwillingness, based on a fear of ill-treatment, which still characterize the Khoikhoi. These travellers utterly failed to get into the confidence of the natives. In justice to our travellers, however, I shall relate what they have recorded.

"By the side of the road," says Thunberg, who travelled in the Eastern Province of our colony, " I observed a heap (stone heap) covered with branches and shrubs, on which each of our Hottentots, in passing by, " threw some branches. Asking them for their reason in doing so, they answered that a Hottentot was buried there. (Thunberg, German edition, i. p. 84, Berlin, 1792.) " Of a certain kind of greyish grasshopper (mantis fausta) the people here believe that the Hottentots offer prayer to it."—(Thunberg, vol. i. p. 68.)

Sparrmann, again, is very doubtful whether the Hottentots after all believe in a Supreme Being. He informs us that, according to the statement of the Khoikhoi themselves, they were too stupid to understand anything, they never heard of a Supreme Being. This, however, does not entitle our author to infer that the Khoikhoi had no God or religion. My experience would lead me to explain what Sparrmann relates. It is a striking feature in the nature of every savage, especially of a Khoikhoi, to pretend the greatest ignorance, though, for all that, one knows that he is very well informed on the subject. It is very trying and annoying indeed to a traveller.

But myths, tales, legends one seldom will get out of a native by questioning. He must be a very intelligent native, with an unprejudiced mind, who will answer at once questions of that kind to an inquisitive stranger, especially if he shows any hauteur.

Our author, however, did not believe in his own statements. He very soon turns against himself, by stating that the Khoikhoi *must* believe in a Supreme, but very powerful and fiendish Being, from whom they expect rain, thunder, lightning, cold, &c.; and he adds that various Colonists had told him *that the Khoikhoi curse at the thunder*, calling him [12] "Gutseri and ǁGaunazi," and [13]throwing something at the lightning and thunder.— (Sparrmann, German edition, p. 196. Compare in the sequel the hymn to the Thunder and to the Lightning with this statement.)

Sparrmann also makes mention of those mysterious cairns. He describes their size to be three to four feet in diameter. This is the general size of those Heitsi-eibib cairns we meet with in Great Namaqualand. He searched in vain in one of those stone heaps for curiosities and antiquities; all he found was a few pieces of wood (p. 549).

The Graves of Heitsi-eibib.

The learned Dr. Liechtenstein, who travelled in 1803 with the Dutch Commissioner de Mist through the Colony, gives a few but very valuable remarks. Liechtenstein and party were travelling in the Eastern Province Outeniqualand, and the field cornet Rademeier was with them to show the road. "The well-informed Rademeier," says Liechtenstein, " who had offered himself to show us the road for some distance, drew, not far from the road, our attention to the grave of a Hottentot, who, according to the general tradition of this people, long before the Christians had immigrated into these parts of the world, had been considered to be a great doctor and a wise man, and whose memory was honoured by the custom, that each Hottentot who passed by threw a fresh branch of flowers on the grave. We actually saw some half-dried branches which might have been thrown there only a few days ago. The grave consisted of a heap of stones about twenty to thirty yards in circumference.

It is interesting that this circumstance, which had not been [14] observed by former travellers, serves as a proof of the higher culture to which the Gonaquas had developed before the other Hottentots, because it was in their country to which this territory belonged. Afterwards we often found such graves towards the borders of Kafirland, but never have I met with anything of the kind in other parts of Africa."—(Liechtenstein, German original edition, p. 349.)

Afterwards the travellers came to the Camdeboo, and Bruintjeshoogte, and Liechtenstein continues his journal, saying: "Before it became dark we passed a narrow spot in the mountain, which is called the '*Israelitische kloof*' (the Pass of the Israelites). Here are various large grave-mounds which are heaped up with stones, and the first colonists in their pious simplicity believed that these were monuments left by the children of Israel who passed here on their wanderings through the desert to [15] Canaan."

Liechtenstein again, speaking of the Ama-||khosa-Kafir, says: "Amongst the ||Khosa there is no trace of a religious worship. They believe in a Supreme Being, who has created the world; but, according to Dr. van der Kemp's assertion, there is no name for it in their language. But they have [16] adopted a name from the Gonaquas (a Khoikhoi tribe) and they call God now *Thiko*. The Gonaquas, however, call him *Theuke*, which word, according to van der Kemp, means '*the one who inflicts pain*,' and from some Kafirs I heard it also pronounced *Thauqua*"—(Liechtenstein, vol. i. p. 410.)

To this I may add, that Edmund Sandilli, the son of the late Sandilli, who is now a prisoner at the convict station in Cape Town, told me that they use *u-Ti* ||*go* for God, a word they borrowed from the Hottentots.

The Kafirs evidently have also taken over the custom of which Liechtenstein speaks, p. 411: "There are spots which nobody will pass without adding a stone, a branch, or a handful of grass. They themselves do not know the reason of this practice; but these spots are very likely the graves of persons of high reputation, whose bodies pious superstition desires to protect from being injured by wild animals; and therefore every one who passes by enlarges the stone heap by adding new stones and branches."

Tsûi-||goab.

Van der Kemp, a missionary, who died at Bethelsdorp (Eastern Province) about 1811, has published a Catechism in the Hottentot language. Unfortunately nothing but the title of it, which was written in the Eastern |Gonaqua idiom, has been handed down to us; and in this title appears the word *Thuickwe*, for God, undoubtedly the same as [17] Tsûi||goab of the Nama, Tsu-||goam of the |Kora, and Tuiqua or Tigoa and Tanquoa of the Cape Hottentots.

Further, Appleyard in his Kafir Grammar, p. 13, gives a short outline of the |Kora language, and notes the name God in Khoikhoi, as follows :

[18] Hottentot : Tsoei'koap.

Namaqua : Tsoei'koap.

Koranna : Tshu'koab, and says in a footnote : " This is the word from which the Kafirs have probably derived their u-Tixo, a term which they have universally applied, like the Hottentots, to designate the Divine Being, since the introduction of Christianity. Its derivation is curious. It consists of two words, which together mean the *wounded knee.* It is said to have been originally applied to a doctor or sorcerer of considerable notoriety and skill amongst the Hottentots or Namaquas some generations back, in consequence of his having received some injury in his knee. Having been held in high repute for extraordinary powers during life, he appeared to be invoked even after death, as one who could still relieve and protect;

and hence in process of time he became nearest in idea to their first conceptions of God."

Tsūi ||goab and ||Gaunab.

Leonhardt Ebner, a missionary who had worked amongst the famous Afrikander tribe or [19] ||Eiχa-||ais, as they style themselves, whose chief was at that time Jager Africaner |Hoā-|arab (Catrib), in South Namaqualand, gives for God the expression *Suquap;* he says it also means a "*sore knee,*" (p. 340). The following are the results of Ebner's researches concerning their religious ideas:—" They did not know of a God, but they believed in a devil, whom they called Gaũab (*i.e.* ||Gaunab). This ||Gaunab fights with an old man, who is much more clever and wiser than himself. Because this old man could not bear any longer the wickedness of ||Gaunab, he made a deep hole and planted sharp-pointed sticks at the bottom of it. And one day this old man challenged ||Gaunab for a fight to this hole; and because ||Gaunab was not as strong as this wise old man, the old man threw him into the hole, where he perished. Rejoicing over this victory, the people slaughtered a big fat sheep."—(Ebner, "Reise nach Süd Africa," Berlin, 1829, p. 237.)

Here I may say that the Rev. Schmelen, missionary of the London Missionary Society amongst the Namaquas, married a pious half-caste Hottentot [20] woman, who assisted him in translating the four Evangelists and a Catechism. For God he always employs, like Van der Kemp and Wuras, the expression Tsoeikwap (*i.e.*, Tsūi ||goab), and for devil 'Kauaap (*i.e.*, ||Gaũäb, or ||Gaunab). This is a clear proof that Schmelen, who spoke the Namaqua language fairly, must have clearly understood from his wife and other natives that, according to their idea, *Tsūi ||goab* was the *Supreme Good Being,* and that *||Gaunab* was his opponent, nay, the *Supreme Bad Being.* We must most sincerely regret that Schmelen has not left some notes on the Hottentot religion to future generations.

My father was an intimate friend of his, and often told me how well acquainted Schmelen was with the customs and manners of the Namas. In fact, he was a white Nama. He was an enthusiastic and zealous missionary, without suffering from fanaticism as so many missionaries do. I believe there is still a manuscript Hottentot dictionary of his somewhere in existence. He himself told my father that he had worked out a comprehensive dictionary with the aid of his wife.

We come now to the worthy Dr. Moffat, the Nestor among the still living old missionaries. He commenced his work in about 1815 amongst the above-mentioned Afrikander tribe, and he also undertook a journey towards the centre of Great Namaqualand.

In his "Missionary Labours and Scenes in South Africa" he says:—"While living among the Namaquas I made many inquiries respecting the name they had to denote the Divine Being, but could not come to any satisfactory conclusion on the subject, though I had the assistance of Africander (the chief) in my researches. The name they use is Tsui ||kuap, or as some tribes pronounce it *Uti'kuap*.[21] .... In my journey to the back parts of Great Namaqualand I met with an aged sorcerer or doctor (|gaiaob) who stated that he had always understood that Tsūi-||goab was a notable warrior of great physical strength; that in a desperate struggle with another chieftain he received *a wound in the knee;* but having vanquished his enemy, his name was lost in the mighty combat which rendered the nation independent; for no one could conquer the Tsūi-||goab (wounded knee). When I referred to the import of the word, '*one who inflicts pain*,' or *a sore knee*, manifesting my surprise that they should give such a name to the Creator and Benefactor, he replied in a way that induced a belief that he applied the term to what we should call the devil, or to death itself; adding, that he thought death, or the power causing death, was very sore indeed. To him, as to many others, this Tsũi-ǁgoab was an object neither of reverence nor love. During tremendous thunderstorms which prevail in that quarter, and which it might be supposed speak to the mind of man with an awful voice, I have known the natives of Namaqualand [22] shoot their poisoned arrows at the lightning in order to arrest the destructive fluid." (Compare the foregoing quotations from Sparrmann.)

It is exceedingly to be regretted that men like Van der Kemp and Moffat, who had an education superior to their brethren, did not succeed in collecting sufficient detailed accounts on the religious ideas of the Khoikhoi. It is painful to think that a certain religious narrow-mindedness prevented them from seeing the spark of true religion and faith which was still left in the heathen's heart. It is indeed advisable for all missionaries to learn from St. Augustine, [23] "*What is now called the Christian religion has existed among the ancients, and was not absent from the beginning of the human race until Christ came in the flesh: from which time the true religion which existed already, began to be called Christian.*"

Missionaries are too apt to treat the religions of heathens as *devil's work*, as *inspirations of Beelzebub*, and they do not hesitate to express this to their converts; nay, they even [24] ridicule and expose their superstitions and religious manifestations. Hence the fear of a savage to communicate the sacred feelings and yearnings of his heart, especially to a man who is sent to destroy them.

Moffat tells us that he had the chief, Africaner, to assist him, and still he could not arrive at a satisfactory result. Africaner was a convert, and how now, if he himself felt ashamed of communicating what he was bound to consider a foolish and absurd superstition. He was a chief, and did not like to make an unfavourable impression; at least, he took very good care not to make a fool of himself.

Heitsi-eibib ‖*Khāb*, ‡*Gama*-‡*gorib*, *Tūsib and* ǀ*Aub, the Serpent.*

Captain James Alexander, later Sir James Alexander, had, no doubt, a very fascinating way of gaining the confidence of the natives. The Namaquas even now speak of him in the highest terms, and praise his social and familiar habits. An old Namaqua said to me of him " ǀAva-khoiï khemi ko tsã ǀhũb ke,"—That man had the flavour of a Redman,—meaning to say that the English traveller knew how to fraternize with them.

Alexander's observations, therefore, we must consider very valuable. He was the first to supply us with specimens of Khoikhoi folk-lore. In these pages we can only reproduce his notes on the mythology and religion of the Namaquas:—

"These Namaquas," says Alexander, "thought that they came from the East. In the country there is occasionally found (besides the common graves covered with a heap of stones) large heaps of stones on which had been thrown a few bushes; and if the Namaquas are asked what these are, they say that Heije Eibib—their great father—is below the heap. They mutter, ' Give us plenty cattle.' "—(Alexander, " Expedition of Discovery," i. 167.)

"There is a strange story about the moon which is a little better than their usual ignorant notions. [25] The moon, they say, wished to send a messenger to men, and the hare said that he would take it. ' Run, then,' said the moon, ' and tell men that as I die and am renewed, so shall they also be renewed.' But the hare deceived men, and said, ' As I die and perish, so shall you also perish.' Old Namaquas will not therefore touch hare's flesh; but the young men may partake of it—that is, before the ceremony of making them men is performed, which merely consists in slaughtering and eating an ox or a couple of sheep."

On the 3rd of August the waggon went on to Aneip (|An-‡eib) or Wetfoot, and I went out of the way, with Jan Buys and two or three men, to see a hole which was supposed to be inhabited by Heije Eibib, or the Devil, and was the wonder of the country."—(Alexander, vol. ii. p. 250.)

Again: "This water-place was called Kuma Kams (Goma-||gams), or the water of the beast tribe, and near it was a heap of stones, eight yards long by one and a half high, *in a cleft between two eminences*, which the Namaquas said was a heap over their deity Heije Eibib (Heitsi-eibib). . . . .

"I turned aside to get water at the fountain, 'Ahuas, or blood (|Aus). In this was said to dwell a snake, which guarded it; but, strange to say, when the fountain was reached it was found to be dried up, and a water-snake, about six feet long, brown above and yellow below, lay dead beside it. The Namaquas immediately cried out, 'Some one has killed the snake of the Fountain of Blood, and it is therefore dried up.' Not far from the Fountain of Blood a young Bushman and his wife was met, and the woman accused her husband of having committed a great crime. She said that the day before they had drank at 'Ahuas, and the Bushman, seeing the snake there, killed it. He excused himself by saying that he was a stranger in that part of the country, and did not know that the snake he had killed at the edge of the water was the snake of the fountain.

"'Ahuas was not the only fountain in Namaqualand which was superstitiously believed to be preserved by a snake. It was singular enough that it should have dried up immediately [26] after the death of the snake.

"[27] Numeep, the Bushman guide, came to me labouring under an attack of [28] dysentery, and said that he was about to die! I asked him what had occasioned the disease; and he said it was from having dug for water at the place called Kuisip, in the bed of the Kuisip River, near our last watering-place, *without first having made an offering*, and that therefore he was sure to die unless I could help him; and I asked him what he meant by saying that he had made no offering at Kuisip.

"'Before any Bushman,' said ‡Numeep, 'digs for water at Kuisip, he must lay down a piece of flesh, seeds of the [20]!naras, or an arrow, or anything else he may have about him and can spare, as an offering to Toosip, the old man of the water.' I asked Numeep if he had ever seen Toosip.

"'No; I have never seen him, nor has anybody else that I know of, but we believe that he is a great [30] Redman, with white hair, and who can do us good and harm. He has neither bow nor assegai, nor has he a wife.'

"'Do you say anything to him when you put down your offering at the water place?'

"'We say, Oh! great father, son of a Bushman, give me food; give me the flesh of the rhinoceros, of the gemsbock, of the zebra, or what I require to have! But I was in such a hurry to drink this morning that I scratched away the sand above the water and took no notice of Toosip; and he was so angry, that if you had not helped me I must have died.'"—(Alexander, vol. ii. p. 125.)

Here we have the most open-hearted confession of a Namaqua (Khoikhoi) who was in great anxiety. The human heart is always more communicative when in sorrow and troubles, especially among savages, whose manners, like those of children, are still very simple and natural, and not dictated by the rules of an absurd etiquette and fashion.

Heitsi-eibib, Kabib, Heigeib, and ‡Gama ‡gorib.

About the year 1842, the missionary work amongst the Namaquas was commenced more vigorously, chiefly by missionaries of the Rhenish Mission. The Rev. Knudsen has left us a translation of St. Luke, up to this date unsurpassed in style and correctness by any other missionary who attempted [31] the difficult task of translating the Bible into Khoikhoi.

Knudsen, however, changed the Khoikhoi Tsũi-ǁgoab into Elob, taking it from the Hebrew Elohim; while for Devil he left the name of the evil-doer ǁGañab. The word Elob is now generally used wherever the Gospel is preached in Great Namaqualand, but it has not supplanted yet the old Tsũi-ǁgoab.

Knudsen possessed a great natural talent both for languages and ethnology. To this it is due that he has provided us with some very remarkable legends, which give us a good insight into the religious ideas of the Khoikhoi; and his notes are of great value, not only because they confirm what has been stated by former travellers and missionaries, but because they have been collected amongst Khoikhoi (the ǀAmas, or ǀAmaquas, of the "Cape Records") who lived in the immediate neighbourhood of the Cape, from Berg river all along the west coast to the mouth of Olifants river. When Knudsen came amongst them they had [32]left the colony just twenty-seven years. The tribe during that time could hardly have exchanged the old Cape idiom for the Namaqua, as, with very few exceptions, they had not intermarried with Namaqua women.

I am therefore justified in saying, that in the following notes we have some religious relics of the so-called Cape Hottentots. Knudsen's account now runs thus: "Heitsieibib or Kabib was a great and celebrated sorcerer among the Namaqua. He could tell secret things, and prophesy what was to happen afterwards. Once he was travelling with a great number of people, and an enemy pursued them. On arriving at some river he said, 'My grandfather's father, open thyself that I may pass through, and close thyself afterwards.' So it took place as he had said, and they went safely through. Then their enemies tried to pass through the opening also, but when they were in the midst of it, it closed again upon them and they perished."

"Heitsi-eibib died several times and came to life again. When the Hottentots pass one of his graves, they throw a stone on it for good luck."

"Heitsi-eibib could take many different forms. Sometimes he appeared handsome, very handsome, or his hair grew down to his very shoulders; at other times it was short again."

"At first they were two (Heitsi-eibib and ‡Gama-‡Gorib). One (‡Gama-‡Gorib) had made a large hole in the ground and sat by it, and told passers by to throw a stone at his forehead. The stone, however, rebounded and killed the person who had thrown it, so that he fell into the hole. At last Heitsi-eibib was told that in this manner many people died. So he arose and went to the man, who challenged Heitsi eibib to throw a stone at him. The latter, however, declined, for he was too prudent; but he drew the man's attention to something on one side, and while he turned round to look at it, Heitsi-eibib hit him behind the ear, so that he died and fell into his own hole. After that there was peace, and people lived happily."

The Death of Heitsi-eibib.

It is said that when Heitsi-eibib was travelling about with his family, they came to a valley in which the raisin-tree was ripe, and he was there attacked by a severe illness. Then his young (second wife, !āris) wife said, "This brave one is taken ill on account of these raisins; death is here at the place." The old man Heitsi-eibib, however, told his son !Urisib (the whitish one), "I shall not live, I feel it; thou must therefore cover me, when I am dead, with soft stones." And he further spoke, "This is the thing which I order you to do. Of the raisin-trees of this valley ye shall not eat, for if ye eat of them I shall infect you, and ye will surely die in a similar way."

His young wife said, "He is taken ill on account of the

raisins of this valley. Let us bury him quickly and let us go."

So he died there and was covered flatly with soft stones, according as he had commanded, Then they went away from him. When they had moved to another place, and were unpacking there, they heard always from the side whence they came a noise as of people eating raisins and singing. In this manner the eating and singing ran:—

"I, father of |Urisib,
Father of this unclean one,
I who had to eat these raisins and died,
And dying live."

The young wife perceived the noise came from the side where the old man's grave was, and said, "|Urisip, go and look!" Then the son went to the old man's grave, where he saw traces which he recognized to be his father's foot-marks, and returned home. Then the young wife said, "It is he alone; therefore act thus:—

Do so to the man who ate raisins to the windward side,
Take care of the wind, that thou creepest upon him from the leeward,
Then intercept him on his way to the grave,
And when thou hast caught him do not let him go."

He did accordingly, and they came between the grave and Heitsi-eibib, who, when he saw this, jumped down from the raisin-trees and ran quickly, but was caught at the grave. Then he said:—

"Let me go! for I am a man that has been dead that I may not infect you!" But the young wife said, "Keep hold of the rogue!" So they brought him home, and from that day he was fresh and hale.[33]—(*Vide* Bleek, "Reynard the Fox," p. 80.)

The evidence of Francis Galton and Charles Anderson on the subject corroborates what has been given in the foregoing, but contains nothing new. I therefore make no quotations from them. During my wanderings amongst the Namaquas, I took much trouble to add to these fragments. Of what I found I shall give the most important instances as condensed as possible.

Tsũi-ǁgoab.

This name is also pronounced Tsu-ǁgoab; this form, however, is the most worn off. Tsū-ǁgoab, Tsũi-ǁgoab, and Tsuni-ǁgoab in Namaqua; and Tsū-ǁgoam, Tsũi-ǁgoam, Tsũi-ǁkhoab and Tsũi-ǁgoab amongst the ǃKora, are forms which have preserved more the original feature of the name. This Tsu-ǁgoab is still invoked almost in the same words as George Schmidt heard it at Baviaans Kloof in 1737. The following hymn is still sung among the ǀGami-ǂnus in the ǁKharas Mountains, amongst the ǁHabobes or so-called Veltschoendragers (sandal-wearers) in the North-east ǁKharas, and by the Gei-ǁKhous, ǁO-geis, and the ǂAunis of the ǀKhomab Mountains East of Sandwich harbour. At the time when the Pleiades first appear above the eastern horizon the people gather for a ǀgei—*i.e.*, a religious dance—and sing the following:—

[31] *Tsũi-ǁgoatse!*
Thou, oh Tsũi-ǁgoa!
Abo-ĩtse!
Thou Father of the Fathers—*i.e.*, All Father!
Sida ĩtse!
Thou our Father!
ǀNanuba ǀavire!
Let stream—*i.e.*, let rain—the thunder cloud!
Ẽn [35]*χuna ũire!*
Let please live (our) flocks!
Ẽda sida ũire!
Let us (also) live please!
ǂKhabuta gum goroö!
I am so very weak indeed!
ǁGãs χao!
From thirst!

!As χao!
From hunger!
Ẽta ³⁵ χurina amre!
That I may eat field fruits!
Sats gum χave sida ītsao?
Art thou then not our Father?
Abo ītsao!
The father of the fathers!
Tsũi-‖goatse!
Thou Tsũi-‖goa!
Ěda sida gangantsire!
That we may praise thee!
Ẽda sida ‖khava ǀkhaitsire!
That we may give thee in return (that is, that we may bless thee).
Abo-ītse!
Thou father of the fathers!
Sida ǃKhutse!
Thou our Lord!
Tũsi-‖goatse!
Thou, oh, Tsũi-‖goa!

If a heavy thunderstorm is approaching, and the country is resounding from the roaring of the thunder, and the lightnings disperse the darkness, they also assemble for a ǀgei, and, while dancing, sing the following:—

ǀGurub di ǀGeis.
The Hymn of the Thunder.

ǃNanumatse!
Son of the Thundercloud!
ǀGari-khoi, ǀGurutse!
Thou brave, loud-speaking ǀGuru!
‡Oũse gobare!
Talk softly please!
ǀHavië t'am u-hã-tamāö!
For I have no guilt!
ǀŨbatere!

Leave me alone ! (Forgive me !)
‡*Oûtago χuige !*
For I have become quite weak—*i.e.,* I am quite stunned, I am quite perplexed.
|*Gurutse !*
Thou, oh |Guru !
|*Nanus ôatse !*
Son of the Thundercloud !

Another song-dance I saw performed in the following manner :—There was a *solo,* sung by a person who played the part of the lightning ; the other part being represented by the inhabitants of a kraal, of whom a member was supposed to have been killed by the lightning.

|*Nabas di |geis.*
The dance-song of the Lightning.

Chorus : |*Aibe* ||*nuris* |*nanuse !*
Thou Thundercloud's daughter, daughter-in-law of the Fire.
Ti |*gãba go* |*gamse !*
Thou who hast killed my brother !
|*Gaĩses gum āb* |*na* ||*goeo !*
Therefore thou liest now so nicely in a hole !
Solo : |*Gãise ta go sa* |*gāba a* |*gam.*
(Yes), indeed, I have killed thy brother so well !
Chorus : |*Gãises gum āb* |*na* ||*goeö.*
(Well) therefore thou liest (now) in a hole.
[36] ‡*Gorob khemi go* |*usense.*
Thou who hast painted thy body red, like ‡Goro !
[37] *Som-*|*auba* ‡*naba tamase !*
Thou who dost not drop the " menses."
[38] ‡*Ei*χ*a*|*kha*||*nabiseb aose !*
Thou wife of the Copper-bodied man !

An old ||Habobe-Nama, by the name of ‡Kχarab, who had great-grand-children, and told me that he had big grown-up children when the Mission Station, Warmbad, was destroyed, 1811, by Jager Afrikaner |Hõa|arab, said to me: "Tsũi-||goab was a great powerful chief of the Khoikhoi; in fact, he was the first Khoikhoib, from whom all the Khoikhoi tribes took their origin. But Tsũi||goab was not his original name. This Tsũi||goab went to war with another chief, ||Gaunab, because the latter always killed great numbers of Tsũi||goab's people. In this fight, however, Tsũi||goab was repeatedly overpowered by ||Gaunab, but in every battle the former grew stronger; and at last he was so strong and big that he easily destroyed ||Gaunab, by giving him one blow behind the ear. While ||Gaunab was expiring he gave his enemy a blow on the knee. Since that day the conqueror of ||Gaunab received the name Tsũi||goab, "*sore knee*," or "*wounded knee*." Henceforth he could not walk properly, because he was lame. He could do wonderful things, which no other man could do, because he was very wise. He could tell what would happen in future times. He died several times, and several times he rose again. And whenever he came back to us, there were great feastings and rejoicings. Milk was brought from every kraal, and fat cows and fat ewes were slaughtered. Tsũi||goab gave every man plenty of cattle and sheep, because he was very rich. He gives rain, he makes the clouds, he lives in the clouds, and he makes our cows and sheep fruitful."

"Tsu||goab lives in a beautiful heaven, and ||Gaunab lives in a dark heaven, quite separated from the heaven of Tsu||goab." I could not for a long time understand what was meant by the two heavens, and could not help thinking that we had here some Christian ideas transferred into the Hottentot mythology. But the worthy Rev. Wuras, of Bethany, Orange Free State, Superintendent of the Berlin Mission, who has been now more than fifty years amongst the |Koras, writes to me in a letter, dated Bethany, Orange Free State, July 9, 1879, that the Koranas always told him *Tsũi||goab* lived in the *Red Sky* and ||*Gaunam* in the *Black Sky*, and those two Beings fought together in former times, and Tsũi||goab received a blow at his knee from ||Gaunam. Tsũi||goam was a great chief and sorcerer among the |Kora, and possessed numbers of cattle. Mothers also used to tell their children to beware of ||Gauna, as he is a great evil-doer, who could kill them.

In the following chapter, where we will trace all the names back to their workshop, we shall see what Tsũi-||goab has to do with the *Red Sky*. The Koranas again say that Tsũi||goab made the first man, and that the snake was together with the first man on the earth. The person from whom the Rev. Wuras heard this was a man far over hundred years of age. Although this note savours much of the second chapter of Genesis, I repeat it here because throughout the Khoikhoi territory the belief is extant that in every fountain is a snake.[39]

To return to Tsũi||goab, I have to remark that, whereever I met colonial Khoikhoi or Namaqua, whether Christians or heathens, the word *Tsui-||goatse* is used interjectionally, as we say, " *good God*," or simply " *God, what will become of me ?*" &c., either as an expression of surprise or anxiety—viz., " *Tsu-||goatse, who will help me ?*" or " *Tsu-||goatse, what have I done, that I am so severely punished ?*" But it is also used as a formula of imprecation, thus:—" Tsu-||goatse, sats |guitsa ‡an, |haviota hã |kheië," " Oh, Tsu-||goa, thou alone knowest that I am without guilt," or " ‡Eīts ta khemi dīre, χavets ni Tsũi-||goaba ‡ an," " Do what you think, but you will know—*i.e.*, find out Tsui-||goab" [that he will see your doings, that he will punish you]. Here we have a very clear instance that Tsu-||goab is looked at as the avenger, similar to the Dawn, Saranyu in the Vedahs. In the following chapter we shall discuss this point more closely, when we enter on the original meaning of the name Tsũi||goab.

Here it may not be out of place to mention an incident I experienced on a journey in Great Namaqualand.

We were on the outskirts of the Kalihari, about latitude 26°, and wanted to go to a Mission-station in westerly direction. The distance to our next water was calculated three days' hard riding with the ox-waggon. We, however, had made the calculation without the host, because, after three days, we found ourselves still another twelve hours from the water. We had only for ourselves a little water in a cask, which, however, was almost consumed. In the night before the fourth day we lost our road, and it was only after some hours that we discovered our mistake. If we had to pass another twenty-four hours like this, not one of us would have seen the next day. Even in the night the air appeared to come from a hot oven. I scolded the guide, a raw heathen from the ǁHabobe tribe, angrily for his carelessness, and asked, " What have you done ? to-morrow we will be eaten by the jackals and vultures. Who will now help us out of this trouble ?" The man coolly answered : " Tsũi-ǁgoab gum ni huidao"—" Tsũi-ǁgoab will help us." I : " What nonsense, you and your Tsũi-ǁgoab are both stupid fools !" He : " Amase ti ǀhũkhoitse, ǁĕib ni hui,"—" Truly, Master, he will help." In the morning, about nine o'clock, we reached the water. After we had quenched our thirst, and were relishing a cup of coffee and a pipe, and talking over our troubles, laughingly, my guide said, " Ti ǀhũtse ǁarits ke ko ǀgamte-ǂgao hã, χaveb ke Tsũiǁgoaba ko ǂkhãtsi, tsĭ ǁeĭb ko nesiri hui ǀkheisa mũ-ǀants ko ǁǀnai !"—" My dear Master, yesterday you could almost have killed me, but the Lord refused you (to do so), but have you now convinced yourself that the Lord has helped?"

We require no further evidence to see what the rawest Namaqua, with all his heathendom, means by Tsũi-ǁgoab.

But still it may not be uninteresting to hear the evidence of another Hottentot.

The famous ǀNanib, who fell so bravely in the battle of ǂHatsamas, when surrounded by the treacherous tribe of the ǁGau-ǀgõas, who simply out of spite made common cause with the Damaras against their own flesh and blood, before he received the finishing stroke, was called upon to turn a Christian, and answered, "*Never;* my Tsūi‖goab is as good as your Christ." He was strongly opposed to missionary work, and considered the missionaries to be a set of mischief-makers. His brother, |Haiguχab or ‡Arisimab, the present chief of the ‖Habobes, is as bitter an enemy of the missionaries as he was himself. With this younger brother I had once a conversation about the origin of his tribe, when he told me: "That very thing, the ‖Habobe, has been made by Tsūi-‖goab in this country, and |Khūb has made us, and given us this country. He gives to us the rain, and he makes the grass grow; and if we ask payment for our grass and water, we do the same what you white people do in asking payment for your lead and powder."

As to Tusib, about whom I quoted from Sir James Alexander in the preceding pages, I have the following from a Namaqua, an old ‡Auni. Very heavy thunder-clouds were towering above the horizon. We both looked with great enjoyment towards the clouds, calculating that in a few hours' time the whole country ought to swim in water. "Ah," he said, "there comes *Tsūi ‖goab* in his old manner, as he used to do in the times of my grandfathers. You will see to-day rain, and very soon the country will be covered by *Tusib.*" I asked him what he meant by *Tusib?* He answered, "When the first green grass and herbs come after the rain, and in the morning you see that green shining colour spread over the country, we say: *Tusib ke* |*hūba ra* |*gū. Tusib covers the earth.*" This reminds one of 2 Samuel xxiii. 4, "And he shall be as the light of the morning, when the sun riseth, even a morning without clouds; as the tender grass springeth out of the earth by *clear shining after rain* or the *splendour of the rain.*"

A second good Being who bears all the characteristics ascribed to Tsūi‖goab is Heitsi-eibib. He is adored and worshipped up to this very moment by the inhabitants of Great Namaqualand and the North-western Cape Colony.

Every Nama from whom I inquired told me that this Heitsi-eibib is their great-grandfather, and a great powerful rich chief. He lived originally in the East, and had plenty of cattle and sheep. Therefore they make the doors of their huts towards the East, where the sun and moon rise. This custom is so peculiar to them that those who possess waggons always put these vehicles alongside of their houses, with the front towards sunrise. All the graves are directed towards the East, and the face of the deceased is also turned to that direction. Heitsi-eibib conquered and annihilated all his enemies, who killed his people. He was very clever and wise, and could foretell what was going to happen in future. Amongst the Bundle-Zwart, or |Gami‡nus, I heard the following story, which I afterwards traced, more or less varied, among the ||Habobes, |Kharagei-khois, and ||O-geis.

Heitsi-eibib's battles with ‡Gama-‡gorib |Haŭ-|gai-|gaib, ‡Amab and the Lion.

Heitsi-eibib lived on one side, but ‡Gama-‡gorib, |Haŭ-|gai-|gaib and the Lion lived on the other side, on three roads, in the middle (between him and his people). There were also people living in the neighbourhood. And these people were Heitsi-eibib's people. Heitsi-eibib sent for them, but he waited in vain. At last he heard a rumour why they did not come. He then started to look after them, and came first to the place of ‡Gama-‡gorib. But he passed and did not call, as a Khoikhoi generally does when he is travelling (and passes a kraal of another). ‡Gama-‡gorib sent his messenger the Hare to call Heitsi-eibib. But the latter gave no answer. Again the Hare was sent, and Heitsi-eibib, following the invitation, said to ‡Gama-‡gorib: " I have come to look after my people." But on the place of ‡Gama-‡gorib there was a hole, and all the people who passed this place were thrown by ‡Gama-‡gorib into this hole, and so they perished. ‡Gama-‡gorib challenged Heitsi-eibib, and said: "Come, let us play the ⁴⁰‡Hī-game."

And first Heitsi-eibib was thrown into the hole. But he spoke to the hole, and said: "Hole of my ancestors, heave up your bottom a little, and give me a lift, that I can jump out." The hole obeyed, and Heitsi-eibib jumped out, and ‡Gama-‡gorib could not prevent it. They played a second match, and Heitsi-eibib was again pitched into the hole, but ‡Gama-‡gorib was exhausted. Again Heitsi-eibib said: "Hole of my ancestors, give me a lift that I may jump out." The hole heaved up, before ‡Gama-‡gorib could prevent Heitsi-eibib from jumping out. And they played a third match, and Heitsi-eibib pitched ‡Gama-‡gorib into the hole, by giving him a dead blow behind the ear, and the air resounded |ap!

And ‡Gama-‡gorib perished there. And Heitsi-eibib spoke again to the hole: "Hole of my ancestors, heave up your bottom, that my children may come out." And the hole raised the bottom, and all the children of Heitsi-eibib came out. And Heitsi-eibib cursed the Hare: "From this very day I curse thee; thou shalt not carry any more messages; thou shalt not eat during the daytime; thou shalt only be allowed to eat during the night, and then only will your voice be heard."

Thus he cursed the Hare, and the Hare ran away into the field, and still runs up to this day."

Heitsi-eibib started for |Haũ-|gai-|gaib's kraal. He arrived there, but he did not greet the master, and passed on. And he was called by the messenger, and that messenger's name was ‡Amab. But Heitsi-eibib refused. And he was again called. The second time he went up to the kraal of |Haũ-|gai-|gaib. Heitsi-eibib greeted the man and sat quietly down. And the man said: "What is the news?" Heitsi-eibib answered: "I have no news." Again, |Haũ-|gai-|gaib said: "Where art thou going to?"

And he answered: "I am going in search of my people." And on the place of |Haũ-!gai-!gaib there was also a hole. And |Haũ-!gai-!gaib had a stone on his forehead. This stone he always gave to people passing his place, and telling them to throw the stone at him; and if they threw the stone at this man's forehead, it jumped back from there, and struck the man who threw it, so that he fell into the hole and perished. Heitsi-eibib was very clever, and knew all this, for he was a great sorcerer. The other then told him to take the stone and throw it. But Heitsi-eibib said: "Shut thine eyes, and I will throw." And when the other shut his eyes, Heitsi-eibib, instead of throwing the stone at the man's forehead, hit him with it behind the ear, and killed him at once. The man fell into the hole and perished. And Heitsi-eibib cursed the messenger ‡Amab, and after he had given him a good flogging he said: "From this day thou shalt not be any more a messenger."

From here Heitsi-eibib started for the place of the Lion, who lived on a tree. He arrived there, but was not called. He passed, and then returned to the tree and asked the white Vulture (!Urikoras), who looked after the house of the Lion: "Where is thy Lord the Lion?" !Urikoras said: "I do not know; perhaps he has gone this way to hunt." The Lion, however, lived on the tree, where he had his nest. So Heitsi-eibib took the fire-drill (doro-heib), and made fire and destroyed the tree. And he said: "From this day the Lion shall not live any more on a tree; he shall now walk on the ground. And thou, white Vulture, thy voice shall not be heard any more from this day." And the Lion had no messenger from that day.

The end of this story is told by the ‡Aunis, in the following version:—The Lion and Heitsi-eibib were, in the commencement, on very good terms. And the Lion's son one day came to the water, where Heitsi-eibib's daughter was, to fetch water. And he insulted the girl. The girl went to the father and complained. Heitsi-eibib said: "I am now tired of the impudence of the Lion and his children, and I am not going to suffer from them any more. They have killed enough of my people. The Lion, however, had [42] wings, and he used to fly high into the air, and when he saw game or people, he came down like lightning from the sky and killed all the cows, and feasted on them the whole night. In the morning he tried to fly home, but on account of being too lazy and heavy from feasting on the meat of the game, he could not fly, and had to walk home through a narrow pass in the mountain. Here Heitsi-eibib lay in ambush, and waited for him, and came unexpectedly down from behind the rock, and cut his wings off. From that day the Lion is without wings, and has to walk on the ground. And since that day there is enmity between Heitsi-eibib's people and the Lion's children.

Heitsi-eibib's Birth.

There was grass growing, and a cow came and ate of that grass, and she became pregnant, and she brought forth a young bull. And this bull became a very large bull. And the people came together one day in order to slaughter him. But he ran away down hill; and they followed him to turn him back and to catch him. But when they came to the spot where he had disappeared, they found a man making milk tubs (||hoeti). They asked this man, "Where is the bull that passed down here?" He said, "I do not know; has he then passed here?"

And all the while it was he himself who had again become Heitsi-eibib.

Another Legend of Heitsi-eibib.

On another occasion people slaughtered a cow. And Heitsi-eibib became a pot. And the people filled the pot with meat and fat, and made a fire. But the pot absorbed all the fat; and when they took out the meat there was no fat in the pot.

Heitsi-eibib's Graves.

His graves are generally to be met with in narrow passes, between two mountains, on both sides of the road. Those who pass by throw pieces of their clothes, or skins, or dung of the zebra, or flowers, or twigs of shrubs and branches of trees, and stones, on those graves. And this they do to be successful on their way. They generally, if hunting, mutter the following prayer:—

>Oh, Heitsi-eibib,
>Thou, our Grandfather,
>Let me be lucky,
>Give me game,
>Let me find honey and roots,
>That I may bless thee again,
>Art thou not our Great-grandfather?
>Thou Heitsi-eibib!

Sometimes honey and honey-beer is left as an offering at his graves. The Namaquas say that if he returns from his walks over the [43] *veldt,* in the evening, he is glad to see that they still honour him.

He gives the Khoikhoi good advice, and tells them how to kill the Lion's children and other wild animals. He also prevents danger befalling men, if they honour him.

Another Legend of Heitsi-eibib's Birth.

On another occasion young girls went out to fetch firewood, and one girl took a |hobe-| gã (a kind of juicy sweetish grass), chewed it, and swallowed the juice. And she became pregnant from this juice, and she was delivered of a son, who was very clever, and she called that boy Heitsi-eibib. And all the other young women came and helped her to nurse the child, and he soon became a big man.

Heitsi-eibib and his Mother.

Once on an occasion the mother and other friends of hers were travelling. And her boy was very naughty and fretful, and his mother had to stop, while her friends were going on. She went on again and carried him, when he again was naughty, and dirtied himself and his mother. And she had to clean him. In this way he went on, until the other women were out of sight. Then he suddenly became a big man, and forced his mother to the ground, and committed incest. . . . . (In Khoikhoi the word is Xai-si, cum matre coït.) After this he again became a baby, and when she came to her mother, she put him down on the ground, and did not take any notice of him. At last her mother said: "Don't you hear your child crying?" The daughter said: "I hear; but let big men help themselves, as big men do."

|Gurikhoisib's or Heitsi-eibib's fight with the Lion.

The first man, whose name is ‡Eiχa|kha||nabiseb, came with all the animals together on a flat rock in the ‡Goũ||gami River to play the "||Hūs-game. ‡Eiχa|kha-||nabiseb had lost all his beads, and said to the Baboon, "Go thou, and fetch all my copper beads which I have in reserve at home." The Baboon went, and when he came to the house of ‡Eiχa|kha||nabiseb the dogs attacked him, and pulled him to the ground. There was the mother of the man, the mistress of the house, but she did not care to interfere, and the Baboon nearly fainted. After a while she called the dogs, and took the Baboon into the house, and put herbs on his wounds, and healed him. She also gave him milk and *⁵uientjes*. He sat awhile and looked round and saw the skulls of various animals as trophies fastened on the poles of the hut. Then ‡Eiχa|kha||nabiseb's mother gave to the Baboon copper beads, and he brought them to the man who played the ||hūs with the Lion. There was the Leopard, there was the Golden Jackal, there was the Hyena, there was the Red Cat, there was the Wild Dog, and there were all the Snakes. All looked at the game. The Baboon delivered the copper beads, and ran away and sat on the top of a rock, and cried down to all the animals, "In ‡Eiχa‖kha ‖nabiseb's house I have seen the skulls of all the animals."

"What bitch's son," said ǀGurikhoisib, "has the courage to drink the thunder-rain-water of ⁴⁶ǀKhubitsaos? Towards the side of ǀKhubitsaos I see the thunderstorm raining." The Lion said: "I shall run towards ǀKhubitsaos, and I should like to see who will prevent me from drinking it?" "I will," said ‡Eiχa‖kha‖nabiseb. And both parted in anger. When it became dark the man arrived at his mother's kraal, and he put his weapons in order; he poisoned his arrows with fresh poison, and he sharpened his spears. And his mother anointed him with butter which had been melted over the fire; she took it from the sacred tub, and she sprinkled sweet-smelling Buchu on her son, and ⁴⁷*gare*-ed him, to encourage him. The next morning he went to ǀKhubitsaos, where the Lion lay waiting for him under a large mimosa tree. At first he let the dogs drink. After they had done drinking he told them to keep watch on the movements of the Lion. And he kneeled down, and he washed at first the sweat off his brows and out of his eyes, in order to see clearly, and then he drank of the water, throwing it with two fingers into the mouth, so that he also could watch the Lion. Since that day all Namaquas when in the *veldt*, drink the waters of the ponds and fountains in this manner. Eiχa‖kha‖nabiseb got up, took his arrows, and drove them into the Lion; he took his spears, and drove them into the Lion; he shouted at his dogs, "Ari ǀkho, Ari ǀkho," and the dogs attacked the Lion and pulled him down. The Lion was exhausted, and could hardly breathe; he was half dead from the loss of blood, which also soiled the water. The Man at last called his dogs, collected his spears and arrows, and went home. And his mother[48] took the *calabash* with sour milk and poured for him, and she smeared him with fresh-roasted butter, and *gare*-ed him:

Gei khois õatse!
Gomas khema gōtse,
Gei ǁgana ǁnauχatse,
ǀAva ǁgotse,
Gei- ǀava-ǁgos õatse!
Ti daië go ātse!
ǂOüse ta go daisi tamatse!

Thou son of a great woman,
Thy body looks like a ⁴⁹cow's body;
Thou big acacia with large branches,
Thou red Bull,
Thou son of a red she-Bull (*i.e.*, of a heroine)!
Thou who drankest my milk!
Thou whom I did not give the breast slowly (*i.e.*, thou whom I nursed very carefully, and gave much milk).

And she sprinkled him with sweet-smelling Buchu.

And the Lion's mother sat up late until the evening-star had set. And she sent her messenger, the Jackal, to ask at ǀGurikhoisib's kraal after her son. And the Jackal went, and when he approached the kraal he heard from afar the melodies of the reed-dance, and the girls singing and praising the deeds of ǂEiχaǀkhaǁnabiseb.

Tiǁāχatse,
Gei ǂnuvisa ǂgomtetse!

My sweetheart,
Thou daring one!

"Aisē!" said the Jackal, "there are great rejoicings! One can smell the fat dropping into the fire; the smell and smoke of the flesh of fat ewes lies over the kraals. And ǂEiχaǀkhaǁnabiseb's dogs can eat fat, and I must tie the belt round my empty belly."

He went back to the mother of the Lion, and told her what he heard, and she said: "Call the Leopard and the Hyena, and let us be off to ǀKhubitsaos. Let them take digging-sticks to dig a grave for my child." And they went; and towards the dawn, when they came near the pond of ǃKhubitsaos the Lion awoke, and he was shivering from the cold, and he raised his voice:

"Aisē'! tū', tŭ tū', tŭ tū' tŭ, tū' . . . . . . dĕrĕ ǁKhuǃnomab ke tā-te, tā-te, tā-te, tā-te . . . . . . hā."

"Alas! tū . . . . . ." (imitation of the Lion's voice) "the Son of the Mimosa" (or, Mimosa-root) "has con———quered me!" (again imitation of the Lion's voice).

He said it with a mournful and tremulous voice, like one who is expiring. His mother said: "Hark! that is the voice of my son." And she went and found him in the agony of death, and his eyes were broken.

And she wept:

"Did I not tell thee, my son,
Beware of the one who walks quite straight,
Who has sharp spears and poisoned arrows,
Whose dogs' teeth are like poisonous arrow-heads?
Thou son of the short-eared one,
Thou yellow child of the Liontail,
Why didst thou not listen to what thy mother told thee?"

And there he died, and they buried him. And they returned again to ǃAvasab; and when they passed the kraal of ǀGurikhoisib, he shouted: "Has the son of the short-eared one not drunk enough of the water of ǃKhubitsaos, that his mother walks alone over the fields?" And the girls of ǀGurikhoisib's kraal said: "No; he has become ill on account of drinking too much of the water at ǃKhubitsaos. It is no water for jackals; only big men can drink that water without taking ill."

Since that day all Khoikhoi will kill the Lion's children wherever they meet them; and the Lion also, if he finds a man unawares, will kill him, to [50]revenge the death of his great-grandfather.

The ⁵'Orion Myth, or the Curse of the Women.

The |Khunuseti (Pleiades) said to their husband, "Go thou and shoot those three Zebras for us; but if thou dost not shoot, thou darest not come home." And the husband went out only with one arrow, and he shot with his bow. But he did not hit, and he sat there because his arrow had missed the Zebras. On the other side stood the Lion and watched the Zebras, and the man could not go and pick up his arrow to shoot again. And because his wives had cursed him he could not return; and there he sat in the cold night shivering and suffering from thirst and hunger.

And the |Khunuseti said to the other men: "Ye men, do you think that you can compare yourselves to us, and be our equals? There now, we defy our own husband to come home because he has not killed game."

What an old Namaqua told me of ||Gaunab.

Some people say thus: The Rainbow (Tsavirub) has been made by ||Gaunab. The Rainbow is a fire which he has kindled. My grandfather also called the Rainbow "|Aib" (i.e., *fire*). He said that ||Gaunab deceives the people, and leads them into that fire, and there they die. And my grandfather said that then people are called ||Gauna-||ō-khoin (*i.e.*, devil-dying-people. These ||Gauna-||ō-khoin we also call Sobo-khoin or |Hai-|nūn (*i.e.*, people of the shadow, or ghosts, fawnfeet, people with a fawn-colour). Formerly the Namaquas used to leave old and aged people in the kraal with some food and water; and they shut the kraal, that no wild animals could enter, and there the people died the devil's death (||gauna-||ō). And such people were not buried, but were devoured by the vultures. Even rich people, who had food enough, getting afraid of the witchcraft of which they supposed aged people to be possessed left them behind in the kraal.

What the same old Khoikhoi told me about the Pleiades.

If the Pleiades set in a thundercloud—*i.e.*, covered by a thundercloud—then they call this cloud the |nū-|auib |nanub. |Nūb is a certain mythological Being, who makes in the winter the hoar-frost, and this hoar-frost they call |Nub di χouba, the excrement of |Nūb.

Superstitions and Charms.

In giving the fragments of the Khoikhoi religion and mythology our chapter would be incomplete if we omitted what we know of the superstitions of the Khoikhoi. No religion is without superstition, and there is hardly a man, be he the most radical freethinker, who, if he only carefully observes himself, would not find that on more than one occasion he has been influenced by superstitious fear. If anything proves that we are linked in an unbroken chain to primæval men, and that our religious ideas are rooted in the past, this fact, that the most cultivated mind cannot rid itself of superstition, should convince us of such a connection.

Goethe, who makes Faust say :

"From faith her darling miracle hath sprung,"

certainly speaks from experience. Superstitions, no doubt, are like belief in miracles, because they do not explain events naturally. And as long as man exists on this earth, and hearts crave for an explanation of the wonderful works of the Invisible, so long will there be religious faith with superstition as her darling child. Even where the religious ideas have been developed to the purest conceptions of the Invisible, the heart clings stubbornly to some old superstition, because we imbibed it with the mother's milk : " No nation has yet completely purified itself from superstition—that is to say, from the remnants of earlier religious notions."

And where the religious sentiments of a race are still

in an undeveloped state, there superstition will manifest itself in gloomy and direful forms. This is actually the case with the Bantu race, where a tyrant rules despotically with an iron rod, by the aid of a wicked set of demoniacal sorcerers. The true religious sentiments in this case are nipped in the bud.

Here, one day, the writer of a History of Culture and Civilization in South Africa, will, I am sure, justify the policy of the greatest statesman who ever came to our shores, which policy consists in breaking the power of the chiefs, and opening to the individual a prospect of sharing in the blessings of civilization. Those who at present cry down this policy, either to gain their own selfish object, or who, from a certain faint-hearted feeling —the so-called Exeter Hall philanthropy—advocate the right of barbarism and heathendom, will for ever be stained with the mark of Cain as traitors to the cause of civilization in South Africa. To train the savage to eat his bread in the sweat of his brow; to teach him to submit to the law, not out of fear for punishment, but for the sake of moral principle; to teach him to respect his neighbour and to love him as the brother who has in common with him the one "great-grandfather"—this is true religion and true philanthropy. It is a work which can be done only in the course of centuries, and not in one day. If it could be done in one day, we should not meet with sorcery, witchcraft, and superstition in native communities, even those that parade in the mission reports as model congregations from whom we civilized Christian races could learn.

Here I give some specimens of superstitions as I found them on mission stations, as well as in the *veldts* among the heathens. It is a curious fact, while the ancient myths may be forgotten and the heathen form of religion may be abandoned, superstitions easily transplant themselves like spores on the new creed, and carry on another parasitical life.

1. At a child's birth a fire is made in the house with the firedrill (dorob). No steel or flint or matches are allowed. This fire is to be maintained until the navel of the child has healed, and the [52]umbilical cord has fallen off. Nothing may be cooked or roasted on that fire. If these points be not strictly observed, the child will die.

2. If a Khoikhoi go out hunting, his wife will kindle a fire. She may not do anything else but watch the fire and keep it alive. If the fire should be extinguished, the husband will not be lucky. If she does not like to make a fire, then she must go to the water and commence throwing it about the ground. If she is tired, her servant must continue pouring water about. If this be neglected, the husband will not be successful.

3. J. Campbell, visiting v. d. Kemp's mission station, Bethelsdorp, in the eastern province, in 1812, says:— 'They (Hottentot women) likewise gave me a piece of something like rosin, which is found on the sea-shore. Before their husbands went to hunt they used to set this on fire, and while the fire ascended they prayed to the *Great Being* for their success.

4. I have already mentioned that throughout Great Namaqualand it is believed that in each fountain lives a snake, and if that snake leave the fountain or be killed, the fountain will dry up. This snake is called the ‡*Gâbeb*, "the one which lives in a hole."

5. If before the commencement of the rainy season snakes move about more than usually, the Khoikhoi say there will be abundance of rain that year.

6. Capt. Alexander tells us in his admirable book, "Expedition of Discovery to the Country of the Namaquas, &c.," vol. i. 115: "Hares I found plenty of at the Orange River mouth; there is also the large eland-buck to be found here; *and an immense snake is occasionally seen*, whose trace on the sand is a foot broad. The natives say that, if coiled up, the circumference of this snake is

equal to that of a waggon wheel; *and when it visits the Orange River mouth, it is a sign of a good season for rain."*

The name for snake is |*au-b* (sing. masc.), and for fountain |*au-s* (sing. fem). Blood is also |*au-b*; bloody, full of blood, saturated with blood, |*au*-χ*a*. According to Khoikhoi custom, as I pointed out in the first chapter, the *daughter* is always named after the *father*. It is therefore obvious that the fountain water |*au-s*, is considered to be the daughter of |au-b the snake. But |*au* originally means *to flow*. And |*au-b*, the snake, or |*au-s*, the fountain, is nothing else than saying, *he flows* or *she flows*. The snake, however, is the one who *flows* over the ground, and in German we say, "Der Fluss oder der Bach *schlängelt sich durch das Thal*" (*i.e.*, the river or the brook *sneaks* through the valley—i.e., *it moves like a snake, winding*). It is now quite transparent that the original meaning of |*au-b*, snake, was *the one who flows*, and was identical with |au-b, blood, which also meant *that which flows*, the "*flow-er*." It does not require an explanation why the blood flowing through the veins should be called the "*flow-er.*" A similar idea connects in the Teutonic languages, *blut*, *blood*, *bloed*, *blôd*, *blôth*, *pluot*, *bluot*, with the Latin *fluvius*, and *fluitare* and *flutare*, although the change of consonants does not appear to be quite in accordance with Grimm's law. (*Vide* Weigand's "Deutsches Wörterbuch, Blut.")

The streaming and flowing of the cloud—that is, the rain —is also derived from the root |au. |Au-ib, or, as it is generally written by the missionaries, |awib (it should at least be |avib), is the rain; to rain, is |au-i or |avi—that is, to be streaming, to be flowing. |Au signifies also *to bleed*, and consequently *to be angry, to have an ill feeling*. Thus one often can hear, |Autsi-ra khoib ke, That man bears an ill-feeling against thee—*i.e.*, that man has been hurt by you, he bleeds, he feels sore, and craves for satisfaction. This phrase expresses extreme pain. We say also, *My heart bleeds.*

The colour red, |ava, also takes its origin from |au, to bleed; hence |ava or |aua, blood-like, blood-coloured—*i.e.,* red.

And at last, *to milk* is also |au—that is, to cause to flow, to make streaming—viz., the milk.

To return now once more to |aub, snake, and |aus, fountain, we see how both words were predicative expressions, saying *he* or *she flows* or streams—viz., the water, which in Khoikhoi can be either masculine ||gami, or feminine ||gams, according to the emphasis of the speaker; afterwards these words become appellatives, meaning the flow-er. And as these words came from the same root, |au, the object which made the greatest impression on the human mind—and this was certainly the poisonous fiery snake, whose bite caused pain, and sometimes immediate death—became masculine; and the soft cooling water, which refreshed the exhausted wanderer, and nursed the trees, and gave life to the plants and herbs, received the feminine suffix. Then, when the original meaning of *to flow* and *to stream* was forgotten, mythology got hold of |aub and |aus, and made sure *that in every fountain lived a snake.*

In German, or, better, in the whole realm of Indo-European folk-lore and mythology, we see, all over, the serpent and the water brought into connection. When Winkelried killed the Dragon, "*a rivulet suddenly streamed out of the hole of the Dragon.*" All legends of dragons and serpents have their origin on the banks of lakes or rivers. We refer to Hercules, who killed the Lernaic Hydra. Apollo kills Python close to a fine flowing fountain, as one of the Homeric hymns tells us:—

ἀγχοῦ δὲ κρήνη καλίρροος, ἔνθα δράκαιναν
κτεῖνεν ἄναξ Διὸς υἱός, ἀπὸ κρατεροῖο βιοῖο·

At the fountain of Ares watched a dragon, who refused water to Kadmos and his followers. In Switzerland, if rivers break down from the mountains after a thunderstorm, the people say: "A dragon has come out." In Denmark Müllenhof found a legend, " that in the spot where once a Lindwurm's (*i.e.*, a dragon's) trail was to be seen, now a brook is ⁶³winding. Beowulf kills the dragon who lives in the lake. Acheloos, the River-god, became a serpent when Hercules fought for Deïaneira. Siegfried kills the dragon in the cavern on the Rhine; and many more instances too numerous to mention. (See on this subject, Schwartz, "Ursprung der Mythologie," Berlin, 1860, especially pp. 58, 59, &c.; Peschel, "Races of Man," p. 252; "On Serpent Worship," Lubbock, "Origin of Civilization," pp. 186, &c.; Müller, "Americanische Urreligionen.")

So much as to the Serpent and Fountain superstition among the Khoikhoi. I have eagerly searched, but in vain, for indications of a serpent worship among the Namaquas, as we find among the Kafir tribes, especially the Ama-Zulu. What I heard and saw with my own eyes amongst the natives may here find place at once.

Not so many years ago a sorcerer died. When he felt his end approaching, he whistled, and all at once snakes of all sizes and of all descriptions came and assembled round their master, and crept over him, so that the eye-witness from whom I have this, and other people who were in the hut, cleared out as fast as their feet could carry them. The same person told me that he had a dispute once with that sorcerer about the power he exercised over the snakes, when the man told him that, if he doubted his witchcraft, he would call as many snakes as he wished to see. Upon which he whistled, and snakes of every kind approached from all directions, and the sorcerer took them from the ground and put them round his neck.

In January, 1872, I was on the mission station Warm Bath (or Nisbet Bath), in Great Namaqualand. I offered payment to the value of three and four shillings for large snakes, especially for very poisonous animals. No sooner was this known than a young fellow, of about twenty-two years of age, came to me and said he would bring as many as I liked, but he wished a goat for each pair. I agreed, and after some hours he returned with a pair of yellow cobras. Not seeing them, I asked, "Where are the snakes?" And he opened the shirt over his chest, where I saw the heads of the two dangerous animals. He took them each by the neck, and I applied a dose of tobacco-oil with a brush to the mouth and nose of each, when they immediately fainted, and were secured in large bottles. Afterwards the same fellow brought me ever so many other snakes, all alone.

On another occasion we were travelling, when a large yellow cobra moved towards the waggon with the intention of attacking one of my bullocks. I immediately grasped the shot-gun, and jumped down from the waggon, when the snake took to flight. I, however, gave her a very good charge in the neck and head; and in her agony she flung herself a distance of more than thirty yards into the bushes. It struck me that my people after this treated me with a certain awful respect, and telling each other, "!gai-aob ke, !gai-aob ke," he is a sorcerer—he is a sorcerer, kept always at a respectful distance. I had some trouble afterwards to convince them of the contrary.

Snakes are also said to be very fond of milk. They go at night to the cows in the kraal and suck there, or even to women in the house. And if a woman refuses they bite her. The same thing happens when a cow kicks them off.

Another snake, the !Ganin-!gub, is said to have genitals, and while women are asleep this snake tries to have connection with them. I was once at a kraal, and the people were in great excitement, and sate up the whole night, because a girl while milking had seen the !Ganin-!gub approaching her. Not a single woman was to be persuaded to go to sleep, and everybody had some weapon to defend himself against the !Ganin-!gub.

Another kind of snake, the ||Huitsibis, is said to live on the forehead of the eland-antelope.

7. To proceed in our account of superstitious customs

and manners, Dapper, in his description of Africa, p. 621, tells us:—" Some of them wear round the neck roots, which they find far inland, in rivers, and being on a journey they light them in a fire or chew them, if they must sleep the night out in the field. They believe that these roots keep off the wild animals. The roots they chew are spit out around the spot where they encamp for the night; and in a similar way if they set the roots alight, they blow the smoke and ashes about, believing that the smell will keep the wild animals off.

I had often occasion to observe the practice of these superstitious ceremonies, especially when we were in a part of the country where we heard the roaring of the lions, or had the day previously met with the footprints of the king of the beasts.

8. The Korannas also have these roots as safeguards with them. If a Commando (a warlike expedition) goes out, every man will put such roots in his pockets and in the pouch where he keeps his bullets, believing that the arrows or bullets of the enemy have no effect, but that his own bullets will surely kill the enemy. And also before they lie down to sleep, they set these roots alight, and murmur, " My grandfather's root, bring sleep on the eyes of the lion and leopard and the hyena. Make them blind, that they cannot find us, and cover their noses, that they cannot smell us out." Also, if they have carried off large booty, or stolen cattle of the enemy, they light these roots, and say: " We thank thee, our grandfather's root, that thou hast given us cattle to eat. Let the enemy sleep, and lead him on the wrong track, that he may not follow us until we have safely escaped."

9. Another sort of shrub is called ṭabib. Herdsmen, especially, carry pieces of its wood as charms, and if cattle or sheep have gone astray, they turn a piece of it in the fire, that the wild animals may not destroy them. And they believe that the cattle remain safe until they can be found the next morning.

10. The root of a shrub called !*Kharab* is taken and cut to pieces, and minced on stones. If one is hungry, he takes the dust and goes to his neighbour's house, where he throws it into the fire, expecting that food will be offered to him. This kind of charm is called the *ho‡ūtes*, or food-finder, food-provider.

11. The roots of a shrub ‡*abus* are also taken and thrown into milk, in order to cause the death of the person who drinks of it. The root is not poisonous at all, and still it is believed to cause the death of a person.

12. Another class of sorcerers, who in former times must have been very numerous, but since the introduction of Christianity are only met here and there on the kraals of the heathen tribes, are chiefly occupied in making rain. Having a great practical knowledge of the meteorology of their country, they pretend to have power over the clouds and to bind them. Thus they sprinkle their urine into a burning fire, being convinced that it soon will rain. They also cut the nails of their fingers, and throw them into the fire for the same purpose. They catch a kind of caprimulgus (‡gā||goeb), and burn the bird to ashes, which are strewn about, in order to produce clouds and ashes. These sorcerers naturally take good care not to display their tricks of witchcraft if there are, according to their own practical experience, no sufficient indications of certain rain.

Throughout the Khoikhoi territory, as far as I could ascertain, the northerly breezes are called tu‡oab—*i.e.*, rain-wind—showing that in the remotest ages the observation was made that the northerly wind was the bearer of rain.

13. Also, if the goats commence to shake their heads and rattle with their ears, it is believed that it will soon rain. It is a matter experienced by every one, that when the weather is very close, the mosquitoes and a smaller kind of flies are very numerous and troublesome. In summer the easterly wind is very close, and as soon as the wind turns

to the north it generally rains. Hence the origin of this superstition.

14. Hunters, especially, have superstitions of their own. If a hare crosses a hunter's path, the hunter will immediately return home; but if the hare runs in the same direction as the hunter's path lies, it is considered a good sign.

15. If a certain kind of chameleon (!aroχab) creeps on a hunter or his weapons, or on anything belonging to him, where he is resting on the road, he is believed to be successful.

16. Also, if the Egyptian vulture (Neophron percnopterus), which we already met in Heitsi-eibib's fight with the Lion, follows a hunting party, and always rests where the party has rested, they are sure to be lucky. On the whole, this vulture seems to be a prophetic bird, and its sagacity is well known from the following story, which I heard dozens and dozens of times all over Great Namaqualand:—If the jackal has discovered an ostrich nest, he will look for the white vulture, and then scream out. The bird now follows him, and as soon as they come to the nest, covered by the ostrich hen, the vulture takes a stone and goes into the air vertically over the nest, from where he drops the stone on the breeding-hen. The ostrich, startled from the sudden cutting pain, runs off. Then reynard approaches, and breaks the eggs, and both he and the vulture have a grand feasting in the most amicable manner.

I myself have never seen it, but I have been assured by very respectable and truthful old Namaquas, and I, for my part, believe it.

17. The Korhaan (Otis Kori), if it does not fly far from the hunter and soon again sits down, is believed to give luck, but if it continues to fly far away the hunter had better return.

18. If a hunter has shot game, and if the bullet does not cause immediate death, the man will throw a handful of sand, taken from the footprints of the game, into the air

which, according to his belief, will soon bring the animal down. A hunter also may not sleep on his back, and pull his legs up, so that his knees stand bent up into the air. If he has done so he is sure to have bad luck.

19. About a future life there are certain indications, from the following sayings :—" That the ⁵⁴ Stars are the eyes of the deceased," and also that the Stars are the souls of the deceased. The Khoikhoi appear to connect " eye" and " soul" in the same way, as is expressed in German, " Das Auge ist der Spiegel der Seele." The eye is the reflector of the soul. There is also a form of imprecation : " Thou happy one, may misfortune fall on thee, from the Star of my grandfather." This proves, beyond doubt, the belief in a life after this.

20. Ghosts and spectres have various names. ǁGaunagu (msc. plur.), ǀHaiǀnugu (msc. plur.), Sobokhoin (com. plur.), and ǀHai-khoin (com. plur.). There is a saying : ǁNaũa ǁgauna ta ni—*i.e.*, I will hear it, if I am a ǁgauna—this means, if I am a ghost, then I will have a better insight into things, which I now do not understand.

Also, if a person has lost something and cannot find it, they say : ǀHaiǀnub ke ǀã, Fawnfoot has stolen it.

21. These ghosts and spectres are believed in dark nights to leave the graves and come to the kraals. They make a rattling noise as if they were dragging skins over rocks and stones in order to frighten the people. This kind of spectres goes by the special name of ǀhausan. They are very mischievous, and their greatest pleasure is to beat people almost to death.

Here we have the key to the original meaning of the word ǁGaunab. He was at first a ghost, a mischief-maker and evil-doer, whose greatest aim was to harm people and to destroy (ǁgau, ǁgou) them. Some people are said to die from the influence of this evil spirit, and these are called ǁgauna ǁōra khoin—*i.e.*, people who died the ǁgauna death, or devil's death. Especially if people are not buried, but devoured by vultures and hyenas, they are also considered ||gauna ||ōra. A man who is killed as a criminal, or who is slain according to the rules of the vendetta, or a slave killed by the master, or enemies killed in the battle—all are left to the animals of the desert to be feasted upon, *so that they will be entirely annihilated*, they are also considered ||gauna ||ora khoin.

There is also a cruel custom among the Khoikhoi, of which I have convinced myself—that is, to leave elderly people to their fate; some food and water is left with them, and the younger folks remove to another spot. Inquiring into the reason of this so repulsive practice, I was told that it sometimes was done by very poor people, who had not food enough to support the aged parents. But sometimes, even if there was food enough, and if people, especially women, who had cattle and milk-cows of their own, gave suspicion that they were under the influence of ||Gaunab, and did secretly mischief by practising witchcraft, they were left to die from starvation. The people, awe-stricken, were almost compelled to fly from them.

It is, therefore, not strange that ||Gaunab, the evil-spirit, is also invoked. They promised him offerings so as not to provoke his anger, as is the case among the ‡Auni-Nama, in the Walefish Bay territory. I am almost certain that, before the Khoikhoi tribes separated, this bad Being, ||Gaunab, was generally worshipped, and is of much older date than Tsūi||goab and Heitsi-eibib. It is strange that the !Gabe-Bushmen, the !Ai-Bushmen, the !Nunin, and especially among these the Hei‡guin (or wooden noses), all know ||Gauna, whom they fear as an evil-doer, while we find no trace of the name Tsūi||goab or Heitsi-eibib. For these reasons I am of opinion that the ||Gauna was an evil demon, known already to the primitive Hottentot race, before there was a distinction between Sān and Khoikhoin. Tsūi||goab, however, was a secondary Being, the national God of the Khoikhoi branch.

22. Another custom, common to Khoikhoi, Bushmen and Berg-Damara—of whom the latter have entirely adopted the Khoikhoi language and manners—is the practice of cutting off a finger. This is done even to new-born children who are not a day old. As all sicknesses are expected to come from ǁGauna, or from his servants, the practitioners of witchcraft, it appears that this custom is a kind of sacrifice or offering to ǁGuana; and we are entitled to conclude that, in very remote times, human sacrifice must have been practised by the Hottentot race.

23. If a woman's or young girl's breasts itch, they say: "My son, my cousin, or some near relation, will soon arrive."

24. If a cow, during the night commences to groan in her sleep, the next morning she is caught, and a piece of skin, just above the nose, is cut, so that it hangs down in the shape of an ear-ring or *ear-drops*. If this be neglected, the owner of the cow soon will die.

25. If a girl becomes of age, or if a wedding is to be celebrated, nothing but cows and sheep-ewes may be slaughtered; and if any other cattle is killed the couple is sure to live unhappy. The fattest cow or the finest young heifer is chased about the place by the young men, and thrown with stones and beaten with clubs, until she is so exhausted and trembling with fear that she allows everybody to come near and touch her. If she still should kick and show fight, it is a sure sign that the marriage will be a continuation of fights and quarrels between husband and wife.

26. The girl or girls who have become of age must, after the festival, run about in the first thunderstorm, but they must be quite naked, so that the rain which pours down washes the whole body. The belief is that they will get fruitful and have a large offspring. I have on three occasions witnessed this running in the thunder-rain, when the roaring of the thunder was deafening and the whole sky appeared to be one continual flash of lightning. This was among the ǃGamiǂnus, on the banks of the Geiǃab

river, among the Gei |Khauas at ||Nuis, and among the ||Ogeis, on the banks of the |Kham river. I am, however, assured that even young converts, if they have become of age, absent themselves to outlying places away from the mission stations, to have their bodies washed by the waters of the thunder-clouds.

27. Also, if a woman during her pregnancy eats of the meat of the lion or leopard, her child will have the characteristics of these animals—ferocity, celerity, swiftness, and strength. They also consider the drinking of lion and panther blood as having influence on the nature of a person or on the child in the mother's womb. A woman lost her temper, and was very cruel to her slave. I spoke to her, and asked whether she did not, as a mistress (lady, geitaras), feel ashamed of herself. She said, she could not help it; I must scold her mother, who once drank panther blood in order to get ferocious children.

28. A great influence is also attached to the power of an imprecation or curse. If one had a quarrel with a Khoikhoi, there is nothing more painful to him than not to be talked to. He will come repeatedly and apologize, until he hears the word "|ūtago," I have forgiven ; and to show his gratitude, he will bring a present—be it a sheep or a cow or whatsoever he may afford to give.

I once had a very unpleasant quarrel with a Namaqua ; perhaps he was more in fun, and it was a misunderstanding on my side. Anyhow, I got vexed, and said : " I shall never forget what you have done, and mind what you are about. I will have my day, too ; do not think that, because I am the only white man here, that you will get the best of me !" He laughed, and thought that I was in fun. I, however, left. A year after he met me on the road in another part of the country ; and when he saw that I greeted his friends but did not notice him, he at once borrowed from one of his mates a cow, and said to me : " Take this, and forgive me; but don't be angry any further—I can't bear it." I accepted his apology, and told him to keep the cow. But he insisted upon my accepting it; because he believed that, as long as I refused to accept his cow, I had not forgiven him. I afterwards made him a present of ammunition, and, as anxious as a Nama is to possess that most precious material, he said : " No ; you want to pay my cow, and I shall not accept it."

My father was missionary of the Rhenish Mission Society in Bethany, Great Namaqualand. The year 1848 was a very lucky year; the desert was a flower-garden, and honey was brought by waggon-loads to the station; but honey-beer (!kharis) was also made in immense quantities, and the new converts very soon had too much of a good thing. The following Sunday my father expressed his indigntion at their drunkenness, and said : " I wish, after you have made such bad use of what the heavenly Father has given you to enjoy moderately, that He never again will give you a year so rich in honey !" Strange enough, up to this date there has never again been an abundance of honey. When, a few years ago, I asked the old chief, ||Naiχab of Bethany, quite accidentally, if he could get me some honey, he answered : " What, you ask me for honey ? and your father has cursed the bees not to make honey. Tell him, at first, to take back his curse and you will again eat honey."

29. The eclipse of the moon is always considered a bad omen. Hunting parties, or an expedition of war, will certainly return home, and they say, " ||Gaunabi ge dahe hã," we are overpowered by ||Gauna. They commence to cry aloud, and say, " torob ni ha, ||ō ge ni," war is approaching, we are going to die. The same is said at the appearance of the Aurora australis, or if the awful tail of a comet is seen in the blue vault.

There are some superstitions of a very recent date, which show that the mythological power is still alive.

30. If the cold westerly sea breeze (huri-‡oab) is blowing,

the Namaquas say : " | Hūb ke ni hā," or " Smaub ni hā," the white man is coming, or the trader is coming.

31. If a cock stands before the door of a house and crows into the house, visitors are expected.

32. If hens try to crow they are caught and killed or chased to death. If this be neglected, the owner is sure to die.

33. If a party goes out on a warlike expedition a crow's heart is burnt and pounded and loaded into a gun. The gun is fired into the air, and they believe that as this pounded heart is blown into the air, in the same manner the enemies will fly and become faint-hearted, and they will disperse like timid crows.

34. Another most powerful charm is the Duba, a substance of white colour, and of the size of a fowl's egg. This duba is generally found in ant heaps. The duba is pounded and mixed with tobacco, and then put into the pipe. If a girl smokes this mixture she will fall in love with the fellow who offered her the pipe.

That these superstitions are of a very recent date is obvious from the fact that the Khoikhoi, only through the white people, have become acquainted with fowls, pipes, guns, and ammunition. Therefore such superstitions in which things, brought from foreign countries, are mentioned, cannot be considered to be common to all Khoikhoi tribes.

In this respect each clan has its own superstition. It is curious to observe that the Khoikhoi have not accepted anything from the Bantu nations, while as regards language and religion, and even customs, it cannot be denied that the Bantu nations, who came in contact with the Khoikhoi, have adopted much which had an improving effect on their original condition. That the | Gona-Khoikhoi in the East greatly influenced the Ama-||khosa ; that these people became less ferocious than the Zulus ; that the rule of the chiefs among the ||Khosa was no longer so despotical as it generally is among the rest of the Bantu tribes—who could deny? Nay, even the short time that the Bandieru, a branch of the Herero, stood under the sway of the tribe of the Gei|Khaua, has left an impression on those natives which manifests itself in softer manners and a kinder disposition towards strangers, if compared with the manners of the more northerly Hereros towards the Kaoko and Ovamboland.

NOTES TO THE SECOND CHAPTER.

[1] There must have been a peculiar-shaped stone fetish, such as Wangemann describes in " Ein Reisejahr in Süd-Afrika," Berlin, 1868, p. 500: " In a great channel, worked by the rain, we found a big granite block, about six feet in diameter and as round as a ball, which rested on a basis of a softer material. This stone the Basuto worship as their God. They dance round it on one leg, and at the same time spit at it. The place's name is *Cha Ratau*, close to Sekukuni's stronghold.

[2] The honourable gentleman had a conversation with some Hottentots, who were on the most friendly and confidential terms with him. They informed him that they worshipped a certain god, whose head was as large as a hand or fist, who had a hollow in his back, who was possessed of gigantic proportions. To him they prayed for assistance in times of famine, scarcity, or in any other calamity. It was a custom that their wives spread on the head of this deity a red kind of earth, buchu, or other sweet-smelling herbs, this being not one of their offerings only, but one of many. *From this it can be seen that the Hottentot worship also a god.*

[3] Almost verbally the same said a Namaqua, who never had come in contact with missionaries, and who led a Bushman life in the mountains west of *Gei|aus* (about latitude 24° 25', and longitude 16°). He said: " |Guruïrao ogu ge |Khūb ta goba, tira mī khoiga;

|gabehegu goma ra." The people say, if it is thundering, the Lord is speaking; He is scolding them.

⁴ As to Valentyn's authority, I may add that he refers to certain documents of the Governor, Simon van der Stell, and to the very learned Secretary of the Dutch Government at the Cape, Grevenbroek, who had written a Latin essay on the Hottentots; all these documents were also put at Valentyn's disposal.

⁵ This is nothing else but the *Tsũi-||goab* worship, as I have identified in the third chapter *Tsũi-||goab*, with the Dawn. It is still the way of the Aborigines of Great Namaqualand to leave their huts with the first rays of the dawn, and to implore *Tsũi-||goab*.

⁶ *Gaunia*, evidently from the verb gou or gao, to rule. I am, however, suspicious that Kolb, who often is careless in expressing the clicks, has understood *||Gaunia—i.e., ||Gauna*, the Bad Being, the demon who is opposed to *Tsũi-||goab*.

⁷ The evil-doer, who fights against *Tsũi-||goab*, is *||Gaunab*, and that insect *Mantis fausta*, is also called *||Gaunab*, both derived from a root *||gau*. As will be more minutely explained hereafter, *||Gaunab* means the destroyer, from the root *||gau*, to destroy; and Mantis is called *||Gaunab*, from the root *||gau*, to show, and is the "*one who shows luck*." Here we have an instance that the same word spoken in a different tone will have a different meaning.—*Vide* Theoph. Hahn, "Die Sprache der Nama," p. 23. The same instance we have in the language of the Mandengas, Steinthal, "Mandeneger Sprache Berl.," 1877, § 34; and in Siam, *vide* Bastian, "Monatsbericht der Köngl. Preuss. Akademie in Berlin," Jan. 1867, p. 357.

⁸ To this I could add, from experience, that I have often observed true gratitude shown to me by Namaquas whom I had helped in troubles either with food, ammunition, or medicine. This convinced me beyond doubt, and will also convince the greatest sceptic, that

the Khoikhoi know how to be thankful, and are very sensible of kindness bestowed upon them.

[9] The *Basler Magazine* of 1816, p. 366, offers some remarks on the Religion of the Khoikhoi, quoting Adams' "View of Religions." But when comparing Adams with Kolb, whose remarks we have given above, there is no doubt that Adams, who never was at the Cape, must have drawn from Kolb.

[10] This journal is contained in " Nieuwste en beknopte Beschryving van de Kaap der Goede-Hoop, nevens een Dagverhaal naarhet binnenste van Afrika, door het land der kleine en groote Namaquas," Amsterdam, 1778. The Expedition started from the Cape of Good Hope on the 16th of July, 1761, and returned safely to the Cape on the 27th of April, 1762. According to p. 50 of that Journal, the most northern latitude they reached was latitude 26° 18'. As their instruments were not very exact, we cannot expect a great correctness of observation; and as every one who is acquainted with the territory in question can learn from Hop's Journal, the most northern spot they reached was the " Ford of the Xamob River," about twenty miles south of the present Rhenish mission-station, Keetmanshoop or Zwartmodder (latitude 26° 32'), thus the corrected latitude of Commander Hop's most northern point should be 26° 50'. Seventy years afterwards Captain Alexander, later Sir James Alexander, who managed to reach Walefish Bay by land, took almost the same route, and crossed the Xamob River at a place ǂNanebis, only a few miles below the abovementioned ford. The grandson of one of the members of that expedition, Jacobus Coetsee, is now a wealthy farmer at Misklip, at the foot of the Vogelklip Mountain, the most northerly station of Sir Thomas Macclear's astronomical survey; and the descendants of Pieter Marais, another member of the same Expedition, are wealthy, and much respected farmers in the town of Stellenbosch.

¹¹ I must remark, that from what I observed and could gather, on the graves of *Heitsi-eibib* branches are thrown only, and not on any other.

¹² *T'gutseri* is nothing else but |*gūtsere*, the imperative form of |*gū*, to go, and therefore means, " Go—thou—please," *i.e.*, " Get away, be off !" *T'gaunazi* is the interjectional form, or, as we should say, vocative of ||*Gauna*, formed by the suffix tse or ze (msc. 2 pers. pron.) ; thus ||*Gauna-tse* means ||*gauna*, thou—*i.e.*, Oh ! ||*Gauna;* and |*gūtsere* ||*Gaunatse* is, " Be off ||*Gauna*," or, in Biblical language, " Get thee hence, Satan."

¹³ The Namaquas nowadays still shoot with arrows at the lightning, and tell him to be off.

¹⁴ The learned Doctor shows by this remark simply that he had not carefully enough studied the works of former travellers, like Dapper, Kolb, Thunberg, Sparrmann, as can be seen from the foregoing pages, where I quoted from them. It will appear from the following pages that we meet these graves (*Heitsi-eibega*) all over South Africa, wherever in pre-historic times the Hottentot race had lived, and that the multitude of these cairns in the East corroborates the opinion, stated by traditions and customs, that the nomadic Khoikhoi, to whom this stone-worship is peculiar, had spread over South Africa, coming from the East. The very fact that those graves are heaps of stones, and not of earth, also serves as a proof that the pre-historic Khoikhoi lived in a mountainous, rocky country, and not in sandy flats like the Bushmen. And the word |*Hō*, rock, which appears in names like |*Hoaχa*|*nas*, " Fountain in the rock," or ‡*Nu*|*hoas*, " Black rock " and |*Ava*|*hoas*, " Red rock," or |*ho-ab*, a single conical granite hill, and |*ho-mi*, mountain (rock), is common to all Khoikhoi tribes, and shows that it was in existence before they separated ; while in the |*Ai* Bushmen (North-west Kalihari) the |*Koān* of the Okavango Dorstveldt, there is no word for stone, because there are no stones to be met with. An |*Ai* Bushman, to whom I showed a stone, and

asked for the word in his tongue, said: " The Namaquas call it |ui, but we have no name for it, because you will not see stones in our country."

[15] This is not a bad specimen of the geographical notions of the South African Boers. A Boer once said that he should like to go to England, but he did not exactly know the *Outspan*, or halting-places, on the road.

[16] How this name may have has been introduced to the Kafirs I have, I think, clearly shown in an essay, The Graves of Heitsi-eibib, *Cape Monthly Magazine*, May, 1878, p. 263, where I say: " The Kafirs, however, on the east coast, who must have made their inroads and encroachments on the Red man's territory at least two thousand years ago, had even a friendly intercourse with the Hottentots; they intermarried with each other, as is evident by the present remnants of the |gonas or |gonaqua tribe." And I can add that every anthropologist at first sight, if he musters a number of N|gika, |Galeka, and ||Khosa, easily will discover Khoikhoi blood in their veins.

Women, on the whole, are said to be more religiously inclined than men; they are the guardians of the language and of the religion of their tribe. The children imbibe with the mother's milk the first accents of the language of the tribe, and with the language the religious ideas. The Germans have the pregnant and beautiful expression, " *Muttersprache*," mother's language. We speak of "*Vaterland*" but not of "*Vatersprache*," and we are well aware why.

The Kafirs are renowned polygamists, and we can well imagine that after having been victorious in a battle, they, according to their custom, may have killed the men, but certainly spared the female prisoners, with the view of increasing the number of their wives, as it is considered a great honour and a sign of wealth amongst them to have a large family.

Now, it will be clear how it was possible that the

children, as they are entirely left during their infancy to the care of the mother, were the medium through which the Hottentot clicks got introduced into the Kafir idioms (Zulu, ||Khosa, &c.); and with these elements they introduced the mother's religious ideas and the name of the Supreme Being, Tsū||goab."

[17] *Vide* Theoph. Hahn, Der hottentotische Tsūi-||goab und der griechische Zeus: *Zeitschr. d. Ges. für Erdkunde*, Berlin, 1870, p. 452.

[18] Here we have a specimen of the blundering I spoke of in the beginning of the first chapter, where I protested against the indiscriminate use of the word *Hottentot*. It is obvious that after the word *Hottentot* has become so deeply rooted it would be difficult to annihilate it. But it must be used either to designate the whole race, Bushmen and Khoikhoi, or it must be simply applied to the Nomadic Hottentot or Khoikhoi. Or, from the Khoikhoi words for Bushmen and Nomadic Hottentot, Sa- and Khoikhoi, we should form, analogous to our "Indo-Germanic," a word Satsi-Khoikhoi, to be applied to the whole race. Missionaries, who live among the natives, and the superintendents of missions at least, should not commit any blunders as regards the ethnological nomenclature. Thus, we read in a mission tract, written for general edification: "*Along the west coast are distributed the various tribes of the Hottentots, Namaqua, Herero, Damra.*"—*Vide* Dr. Wangemann, "Maleo und Sekukuni, Ein Lebensbild aus Süd Africa," Berlin (1868), p. 53. That the Herero, a Bantu nation, suddenly were transformed into clicking Hottentots I had to learn from Dr. Wangemann.

[19] ||Eiχa||ais .... This tribe is a branch of the !Amas (the Amaquas of the Cape Records) who formerly inhabited the country between Bergriver and Olifants river. The !Amas again were a branch of the |Khauas (Cauquas of the Records) whose head-quarters were in the Worcester district, the present Goudini. It appears that the greater

number of the so-called Cape Hottentots were tribes who were more or less connected with the |Khauas, and acknowledged that tribe as the paramount tribe, as about fifteen or twenty years ago the Gei||khous of Great Namaqualand had the supremacy over all the Nama tribes. Certain it is that the Gei||khous once ruled from the borders of Ovambóland to the mouth of Olifants river, and that all the tribes of Great and Little Namaqualand sent annually a tribute to the paramount chief, generally consisting of a heifer, buchu, spears, and copper or iron beads, and milk-tubs. The last tribute of that kind was paid in 1863; and in 1856, even from Korannaland the chief Poffadder came to do homage to ||Oasib on‡Hatsamas, acknowledging that his tribe, the "Springbucks," were a branch of the Gei||khous.

To return to Jager Afrikaner and his tribe, the ||Eiχa-||ais, they formerly occupied the valleys of the Upper Olifants river and the Upper Breede-Rivier, in the vicinity of the Witsenberg, a mountain named after Witsen, the famous burgomaster of Amsterdam. Early in the Cape Records, in Simon van der Stell's time, we meet a chief of that vicinity by the name of Harramac, which is |Hara-mub, as no name or word in Khoikhoi ends in c or k. And we meet this name again among the chiefs of the ||Eiχa||ais. This justifies the conclusion that the Harramac of the Cape Records was an ancestor of the ||Eiχa||ai-chiefs. The following names have still come down to us: Tsaüχab, about 1720; |Garuχab, about 1750; |Garuχamab, about 1780; |Hõa|arab geib, 1790–1823; |Haramūb geib, 1823–1861; and |Hõa|arab or Jan Jonker, 1861. .... It appears that their love for freedom was the reason that they left their native hills and dales, under the rule of the old chief |Garuχamab, and went to the north as far as the |Hantam, where they in some way or other came under the sway of a Boer Pienaar, living on the Groot Doornberg farm, near the present Calvinia. Pienaar's unjustice, however, was so provoking that he was killed by the Afrikaners, as the ||Ei𝜒a||ais were styled by the Boers; and under the guidance of |Garu𝜒amab's son, Jager Afrikaner |Hõa|arab, they fled with the Boer's flocks and ammunition towards Griqualand, and from there again all along the Orange River to South Namaqualand, where they settled at ||Hamis or Blydeverwacht. Here the German missionaries, the brothers Albrecht, and afterwards Moffat and Ebner, came in contact with the tribe, who embraced Christianity. Jager Afrikaner died in 1823, and his second son, |Haramub, the famous Jonker Afrikaner, called by the then paramount chief of Great Namaqualand, Gameb, started with one part of the tribe towards the north, against the Herero, who encroached upon the Namaquas, and, with few exceptions, conquered and enslaved them. With Jonker |Haramub's death, however, the late Andersson and Green, and other Europeans, were the cause that the Herero rose, and in a war of nearly ten years, reconquered their freedom. The present chief is |Hõa|arab, son of the late |Hara|mūb. Since 1842, after the visit of Captain Alexander, with a short interruption, they had a permanent mission station at |Ai||gams, at the foot of the gigantic Auäs mountains in North Namaqualand. Space does not allow us here to go into particulars, but this much we can say, that the history of this ||Ei𝜒a||ais tribe would fill the most interesting pages of South African history, not lacking in romance, and recording deeds of which our mediæval knights need not be ashamed.

[20] *Half-caste Hottentot women.*—The title of this valuable translation is: " Annoe Kayn hoeaati Nama-Kowapna gowayhiihati. Diihiiko Hoekays na Kaykoep Bridekirk, kipga. 1831;" or, written with the letters of the standard alphabet, |Anu |gai‡hoati Nama gobab |na 𝜒oahēhāti. Holy good news, Nama language in they have been written. Dīheko ||Hu|gais |na gei|Khub Bridekirkib 𝜒a. Printed Capetown in, great-man (*i.e.*,

Mr.) Bridekirk by, 1831. When this pious woman had just looked over the last proof-sheets, she said, " My task is done, I feel my end is near." She returned with her husband, Mr. Schmelen, to her country, Little Namaqualand. They were, however, not far from the Cape, in the neighbourhood of Melks farm, close to the river Berg, when she was taken suddenly ill and died. Her grave is not far from the western slopes of Piquetberg.

[21] I am afraid that Moffat has allowed himself to be misled, by saying that some called God U-tigoab. He appears to have heard something of the Kafir U-Ti∥go, where U is the prefix masc. The Khoikhoi language does not employ prefixes.

[22] *Shoot their poisoned arrows.*—The Urjangkut, a tribe belonging to the black Tatars, used to scold at the thunder and lightning to drive it away.—A. Bastian, *Zeitschrift für Ethnologie*, 1872, p. 380.

[23] August. " Retr." 1. 13. " Res ipsa quae nunc religio Christiana nuncupatur, erat apud antiquos, nec defuit ab initio generis humani quousque Christus veniret in carnem, unde vera religio, quae jam erat, coepit appellari Christiana."—Max Müller, " Chips," vol. i. xi.

[24] *They even ridicule.*—The following extract, taken from a German Mission Tract by Dr. Wangemann, Superintendent of the Berlin Missionary Seminary, will serve as a specimen of the information given to the European public concerning the religious emotions of the savage, and how prejudice is excited against him:—" The Bible, the word of the Almighty Lord, is so full of wisdom, beauty and truth, that a simple child and the greatest *savant* will find satisfaction and pleasure in it. But it is different with the legends of all the heathens. They are full of absurdities and silliness, and also so full of filth and dirt, that one soon sees they only say what man in his stupidity thought to be nice and agreeable, and what he, in his sinful ideas, invented about a self-made god. Thus it is with the fables of the Basutos. *They are not worth knowing.*"

—Dr. Wangemann, "Lebensbilder aus Süd Afrika," vol. i., p. 82, Berlin, 1871.

If the heathens were as black as they are painted here by Dr. Wangemann, there would be no base of operation for the missionaries in the heart of the savage, and all that they boast of the progress of the Gospel among the heathens would be untrue. Does the prophet not say: " Can the Ethiopian change his skin, or the leopard his spots? then may ye also do good that are accustomed to do evil? Jeremiah xiii. 23. And how will our author then explain to us what St. Paul says to the Romans i. 19: "Because that which may be known of God is manifest in them; for God hath showed it unto them?"

We hardly can believe that Dr. Wangemann is as ignorant about the savages as he, according to the above statement, appears to be. If this be the case, the sooner he cedes his position to a more enlightened man the better. But if he is well informed, and we have no reason to doubt this, we must presume that he blackened the heathens simply to make the success of his mission work appear in a whiter light. It is very painful to us to charge Dr.Wangemann with this stratagem, which, pharisaical as it is, does not do credit to a director of Missions.

[25] There is an almost direct coincidence between this Khoikhoi myth of the moon and one among the Fijians, which is very strange. And still we are not justified in concluding that the one nation has borrowed it from the other. "Two gods," the Fijians relate, "disputed whether eternal life should be conferred upon mankind. Ra-Vula, the moon, wished to give us a death like his own; that is to say, we were to disappear and then return in a renewed state. Ra-Kalavo, the rat, however refused the proposal. Men were to die as rats die, and Ra-Kalavo carried the day." The temptation is great to explain the coincidence of decisive strange customs and peculiar

legends, by supposing that the people among whom they are found descended from a common ancestry in primordial times. But such coincidences merely corroborate the old maxim that among different varieties of men, in different regions, and at different times, the same objects have given rise to the same idea.—Peschel, "Races of Man," London, 1876, pp. 461 and 462.

[26] *After the death of the snake.*—I shall hereafter, in the third chapter, come back to this superstition, and only now mention that the words, |au-b snake, |au-b blood, |au-s fountain, |au to bleed, |au to flow, |au to bear ill-feeling, |avi (from |auï to stream) to rain, |ava red, are all derived from the root |AU to flow, to stream, and we shall see why it is that in every fountain there is a snake.

[27] Alexander is mistaken if he calls ‡Numeep a *Bushman*. The name of this so-called Bushman proves sufficiently that he was a Khoikhoi. The ‡Auni tribe live in the territory here spoken of. The poor Namaquas are also called by the others, Bushmen, especially when they are servants, or if they lead a Bushman's life, and have no cattle and sheep.

[28] *Labouring under an attack of dysentery.*—Sometimes the brackish water works so strongly on the bowels that one who drinks it is immediately taken ill.

[29] |*naras.*—This fruit is a Cucurbitacea, almost as large as a newborn child's head. The flesh of it is eaten raw, and the seeds are kept for the dry season, when there is no fruit. The seeds taste almost like almonds, and are at present to be got from confectioners in Cape Town. The Topnaars or ‡Aunis of Walefish Bay and Sandwich Harbour, and all the Bushmen tribes along the coast of Great Namaqualand, live partly on this fruit. It is to be met with from the Orange River mouth as far as latitude twenty-one degrees: but it grows only on the sandy coast.

[30] *Redman,* or |Ava-khoib, is identical with Khoikhoib,

while the Europeans are called |Uri-khoin, white men, and the Bantu ‡Nu-khoin, black men. For Toosip, or Tusib, see the third chapter.

³¹ *The difficult task of translating the Bible.*—I mention this the more, as I had not long ago the opportunity of convincing myself that a missionary, in a farewell circular, had assured to his brethren, that "*he was the only man who was destined by the Lord to give the Khoikhoi the Bible in their language.*" What I have seen of the publication of the said missionary does not corroborate this opinion, and I can state that his publications require much polishing in style and grammatical correctness.

³² *They had left the colony.*—The mission station, Bethany, in Great Namaqualand, was founded by the Rev. Mr. Schmelen in 1814, who left with about three hundred |Amas the station Pella in Bushmanland, and trecked north until they came to the beautiful fountain |Ui‡ganis on the banks of the ||Gõa|gib River. The |Amas bought the rights of this place and neighbourhood from the then paramount chief of Great Namaqualand, *Gameb*, for axes, knives, iron spears and tinder-boxes; and Schmelen gave the place the new name, Bethany. Amongst the leaders of the |Amas were the Xam|hã (Lion tail) and |Hõa|ara (Cat rib) families, or, as they are now styled, the Amraals and Boois. Their language is the one in which Knudsen's St. Luke is translated, and we have in this way an excellent specimen of the old Cape Hottentot idioms. In 1850 they told my father that they were called upon by the Dutch Government in 1805 to fight against the English. The Namaqua, according to the Cape Records, lived in 1665 as far South as the Olifants river. They have always been, and still are, by far the most powerful tribe among all the Khoikhoin.

³³ At first sight this myth shows some resemblance to the words of the Lord to Adam: "Of every tree in the

garden thou mayest freely eat: but of the tree of the knowledge of good and evil, thou shalt not eat of it; for in the day that thou eatest thereof thou shalt surely die," Genesis ii. 16, 17; and Adam still partaking of the forbidden fruit, died. I heard the same myth on the outskirts of the Western Kalihari, where I met ostrich hunters from the ||O-geis tribe who never had a missionary, and almost every ‡Auni of the |Khoma Mountains and every Gei||khau knows it too. I myself have eaten of the fruit of the so-called wild raisin tree, or ‡oŭs, and the consequence was that I had an attack of dysentery. The natives having no medicine often succumb to such attacks. It is besides a well-known fact, that the flowers and herbs at a certain time of the year prove detrimental to cattle and sheep. Various diseases break out, known by our colonists as *galziekte* and *bloedziekte*. Sometimes cattle suddenly swell up and die, and the natives then remove to more healthy spots.

[34] This hymn of Tsūi||goab, compared with George Schmidt's statement, which we gave in one of the preceding pages, shows us that Tsūi||goab was invoked by all Khoikhoi with the same prayer, in the same way as we now a days all over the world invoke "the Father in Heaven" with the "Lord's Prayer," which Christ taught his disciples. At the same time this hymn confirms the fact, "that a poetic form is more easily remembered than a prose form, and that it is better adapted for securing the strict accuracy of historical myths." I am of opinion that the greater part of the Khoikhoi myths, especially those which tell us of the heroic deeds and fights of Heitsi-eibib and Tsūi||goab, were all in a poetic form, of which such verses as are here and there interwoven in the prosaic parts of the present myths are fragments. For the last fifteen years these epical myths have been sung and performed exactly in the same way as the "Songs of Sanaχab and Gei|aub," men who distinguished themselves in the late Namaqua and Damra war.

I was present at one of these ceremonies, and an old Namaqua told me that, in his young days, Heitsi-eibib and Tsūi‖goab were honoured in the same way.

One sees the whole fight, in which dancers and pipe-blowers are actors. We see the cows and sheep driven off by the horsemen, and we see them retaken; at last the daring and plucky Gei|aub receives a mortal wound by a bullet of the enemy. They strip him naked, and leave him a prey to the vultures, which soon approach and commence to devour the body. At last, the friends having slain the enemy, return and collect his bones in a grave, and sing a very doleful burial song.

[35] χurina, χuna ... χurina (plur. com. obj.), from the singular form χuri-i, are roots, berries, honey, and bulbs, food which is found in the field. The bulbs are called also |hani, and a long mountain range in Central Namaqualand is called after the |han, the |Han-‡ami Mountains,—*i.e.*, the Bulb Mountains. In Colonial Dutch these bulbs are called *Uientjes*. The |Han-‡ami or |Han‡ama Mountains are the same which Captain Alexander wrongly spells 'Unuma. Xuna (plur. com. obj.), however, from singular χuï, means simply things, and in this case it means cattle and sheep; in Colonial Dutch, *vee, groot vee,* and *klein vee.* χurina and χuna evidently have the same root, χu, which means "*something,*" a thing which has a concrete substantial origin, while |kheis is abstract, and means matter, German *Umstand, Sache.*

[36] ‡Gorab is ochre, red clay.

[37] Som-|aub is the "menses."

[38] ‡Eiχa|kha‖nabiseb is the other name of |Gurikhoisib, the Khoikhoi Adam. ‡Eiχa, from ‡ei, copper, is copperlike, full of copper, copper-coloured, brass-coloured. |khāb is body and ‖nabiteb is the backbone (*Rückgrat* in German). The thunder-cloud has often a brazen colour, a sulphur tint. Here one can see how mythology and ancestor-worship flow into one another. Here ‡Eiχa|kha-

‖nabiseb is identical with ǀNanub, the thunder-cloud—
i.e., with Tsūiǁgoab; and in another myth he changes
names with ǀGurikhoisip, the ancestor of the Khoikhoi.
We shall have to recur in the third chapter to these
names again.

²⁹ We shall see more particularly in the third chapter that
ǀaub the snake, and ǀavib the rain, come from the same
root ǀau, to flow. If there is plenty of rain, the fountains
will flow very strongly. In every fountain again there is
said to be a snake, hence the natives say, if the snakes go
much about—that is, if the fountains flow very abundantly
—then it will be a good year. Tsuǁgoab, the ancestor of
men, the creator of the Khoikhoi, lives in the thunder-cloud,
where he causes the cloud *to* ǀ*au*, to stream—that is, he
causes the water-snake to come down. Thus the ǀKora
say, that the snake and the first man originally lived
together. Here I may at once add a note, which I forgot
to give in the text. This remark very likely also comes
from Wuras:—

"There is hardly a trace of religion to be found among
the Korana; but the old people say that they have heard
from their grandfathers that Tsūi-koab had made two
persons, a man *Kanima*, ostrich feather, and a woman,
Hau na Maos, yellow copper. He gave them cows, whose
milk they should drink, a jackal tail to wipe the perspira-
tion off the brow, a staff with a club (kiri), a quiver with
arrows, and a bow, and a shield. From Tsūiǁgoab they
expect all the good things. He lives at the other side of
the blue sky, in a light sky. They also talk of a Kau-
naam, who is an evil-doer. They fear him very much."
(*Vide* Burkhard, "Die Evangelische Mission," vol. ii.
p. 71) Bielefeld, 1860. It should be noticed that we have
here again *Yellow Copper*, which is identical with ǀNabas,
or ǀNanus, the wife of ǂEiχaǀkhaǁnabiseb.

⁴⁰ The ǂHī-game is an old kind of duel amongst the
Khoikhoi. If a man takes offence, he challenges the

other man by taking a handful of dust, and holding it out to his adversary. The enemy then beats the challenger on the hand, so that the dust falls to the ground, and the challenge is accepted. If the other is a coward, he will not beat the dust to the ground, and then the one who made the challenge throws the dust into his face. In duelling together two men try to kick each other, or to knock each other down by fencing with knobkirris, or to throw each other with spears, covering themselves the meanwhile with their shields. This kind of duelling was called ǂhĭgu.

[41] For this reason the Namaquas pretend not to eat the flesh of the hare. The fact, however, is, that they believe, by eating hare-flesh, they will become as faint-hearted as a hare. They, for instance, eat the flesh of the lion, or drink the blood of the leopard or lion, to get the courage and strength of these beasts. The same custom we find among the Malays, Polynesians, and Indians of America, and other savages who drink the blood of wild animals or slain enemies, in order to become ferocious and courageous as they are.

[42] *The lion, however, had wings.*—Ctesias, "De Rebus Indicis," speaks of griffins in the following way:—" There is also gold," he says, " in the Indian country, not found in the streams and washed, as in the river Pactolus ; but there are many and great mountains, wherein dwell the griffins, *four-footed birds of the greatness of the wolf, but with legs and claws like lions.*—Ctesias, " De Rebus Indicis," 12 ; according to Tylor, " Early History of Mankind," p. 318, Herodotus repeatedly mentions these griffins (Γρύψ), iii. 116; iv. 13, 27, 79, 152.

[43] *Veldt,* or, in proper Dutch, *veld,* means the fields, the uncultivated grounds, the grazing-grounds and sheep-walks.

[44] ‖Hūs-game literally translated is *the cloud-game,* from ‖hūs, an antiquated word for cloud. This ‖hūs game is also called ǀkhoros, a kind of *dice.* Why is the ǀkhoros called ‖hūs ? Here we have again metaphor. When the battle in the clouds is fought,

between Tsūi‖goab and ‖Gaunab, or ǂEiχa|kha‖nabiseb and the lion, we see the lightnings—*i.e.*, the *dice* of Tsūi‖goab thrown to the earth. And this phenomenon in Nature, the lightnings dropping to the earth, have afterwards given rise to the story of |Gurikhoisib or ǂEiχa-|kha‖nabiseb playing at dice with the lion. In our legend the thunderstorm is expressly mentioned.

⁴⁵ *Uientjes*, the Colonial Dutch expression for the various kinds of eatable *bulbs*. It means onions.

⁴⁶ |Khubitsaos—lat. 23° 29', long. 16° 28'. I have been to the spot. It lies on the southern slopes of the |Khoma Mountains of the highlands of North Namaqualand. There is a pond of about fifty yards in length and fifteen in breadth. On the banks of the pond grow mimosa bushes; and on the south corner, about five yards from the water, is a very old mimosa tree. I had a man of the Gei|‖khau tribe with me, by the name of Doūsamab. It was quite interesting to see how he pointed the spot where the lion lay, where |Gurikhoisib kneeled and cooled his face with water, where the dogs made the first attack on the lion, &c. The good fellow got quite excited and warm when he saw that I took a great interest in the matter; the more so when he afterwards saw me taking observations in order to fix the place on my map. In |Khubitsaos, or, as it also is pronounced, |Gubi-tsoas, we have again the root |gu, *to cvoer*. In the third chapter the meaning of |gurub will be found, according to this root, to signify the coverer (Sanscr. Vritra).

⁴⁷ *Gares* is an extemporized love song; Khoikhoi mothers, or nurses, are in the habit, while washing or anointing a child, suddenly to extemporize a song of praise, and this way of praising is called *gare*.

⁴⁸ *Took the calabash with sour milk.*—Calabash, from *calebasse*, Sp. *calabaza*, Sicilian *cara vazza*, Portg. *calabaça* and *cabaça*, from the Arab *garah*, a kind of gourd, and *aibas*, f. *aibasah*, dry, so that it signifies a *dry gourd* scooped

out, in which *milk* and other drinkables are carried. The Khoikhoi use the calabash also for churning purposes, and produce butter by shaking the calabash. In Namaqua the calabash is ābas; the root is ā, to drink, consequently ābas, the tub for drinkables, German *Trinkgeschirr*. One place is called *Ababis*, on account of calabashes growing there in abundance. In Spain these calabashes serve as wine vessels, and are called either *calabaza* or *calabacino*.

[49] *Thy body looks like a cow's body*, means thou hast a beautiful, fine, fat body.

[50] How strong the belief is among the Khoikhoi that animals even are revengeful, can be seen from the following historical fact:—When the !Amaquas had settled at Bethany, they went out to shoot the Hereros or Cattle Damaras, and to rob them of their cattle. Once they had a wholesale massacre amongst the Damaras. One man especially distinguished himself by extraordinary bloodthirstiness and cruelty. They had returned home, when after some time a black lion came and took that man out of his hut, tore him to pieces and killed him. The distance from Bethany to Damaraland is about 250 miles. Still up to this day the !Amas believe that that black lion was a Damara who had taken the shape of the beast, and had come that distance in order to revenge his people. Also of elephants and snakes, especially of the so-called dassies-adder, it is said that they can detect the criminal among hundreds of people, and kill him, without turning their ire on anybody else.

[51] I have called this legend the Orion myth, because most of the stars belonging to the constellation Orion act a certain part in it.

In the sequel of the third chapter I shall give an explanation of the names and the meaning of this myth. The Aldebaran, or *a* Tauri, is the aob of the myth, and |Khunuseti, or the Pleiades are his wives. His bow is π π Orionis; his sandals, ǁharon, are ε and δ of the Hyades; his kaross is ϑ and γ of the Hyades; δ, ε, ζ Orionis, are the zebras, ǃgoregu, Leo is the lion. The arrow ‡ab is marked by i, d, c, Orionis, of which again it is called ǁǀnaus, the arrowhead, and c is the opposite end, where ǀams, the feather is fixed. It is very strange indeed that the Pleiades, the rainstars of the Khoikhoi, stand so close to the Hyades, the rainstars of the ancient Greek. And that Orion among the Greeks, as well as among the Khoikhoi, served as a base for a myth of a hunter. Certain it is that the Hottentot myth is of very old date, as the ǀKora, for instance, had still, in Burchell's time, the same names ǀKhũseti for the Pleiades, and ǃgoregu for Orion. And another Khoikhoi tribe, the Geiǀkhauas, who formerly lived in the immediate neighbourhood of the Cape, have still these names and the same version of the above-mentioned legend.

The Namaquas call the stars the eyes of the deceased. One star is ǀgõaros, the little daughter; α and β Centauri are called mũra, the two eyes. (Whose eyes? certainly of some being; and here we have a remnant of an old myth.) Then μ 1 and 2 Scorpionis are called Xami di mũra,-i.e., the eyes of the lion. There seems to be another lion in the Orion myth. Venus has various names, one is ‡onob, *the man with the fingers cut off*. The New Zealanders believe the Pleiades to be men with one eye (Bastian). And in Australia, according to Ridley, the Pleiades are called worrul—i.e., bee's nest. In Greenland the Pleiades represent dogs chasing a bear (Bastian). And among the Bambaras, Bapedis, and Amaǁkhosa, the Pleiades are the messengers of the rainy and planting season. The Indians of North America believe these stars to be dancers.

[52] It is interesting to see how widespread is the superstition connected with the umbilical cord of a child. After the cord has fallen off the New Zealanders place it in a mussel—that is to say, in the same shell with which

it had been separated from the mother—and put the umbilical cord with the mussel on the water of a river. If these things remain above the water and do not sink the child will be lucky; if, however, the mussel capsizes it means early death, &c. (Hooper, in *Journal of the Ethnological Society*, 1869-72). The Alfurus in Celebes keep the umbilical cord, with great care, as a charm (F. W. Diedrich). The Kalmoucks in Asia use it as a charm in lawsuits (R. Krebel " Volksmedicin," p. 56). In Germany the umbilical cord is pulverized and given to a sick child as medicine (M. R. Buck, " Medic. Volksglauben aus Schwaben," 1865, p. 56). And Fischhart says in " Gargantua," cap. 39, of the cowardly soldiers who took to flight : " Etliche zogen ihre Kinderpelglin herfür, meinten, also dem Teufel zu entfliehn." For more contributions on this subject, *vide* Ploss, " Die Glückshaube," &c., in *Ethnolog. Zeitschrift*, 1872, iii.

[53] In Syria also, at the spot where Typhon went into the ground, the river Orontes took its origin : φασὶ δὲ τυπτόμενον τοῖς κεραυνοῖς (εἶναι δὲ δράκοντα, namely, Typhon) φεύγειν κατὰ δύσιν ζητοῦντα τοῖς μὲν ὁλκοῖς ἐντεμεῖν τὴν γῆν καὶ ποιῆσαι τὸ ῥεῖδρον τοῦ ποταμοῦ, καταδύντα δὲ εἰς γῆν ἀναρρῆξαι τὴν πηγήν, ἐκ δὲ τούτου γενέσθαι τοὔνομα τῷ ποταμῷ· — Strabo, C. 751, e. *Vide* Schwartz, " Ursprung der Mythologie," Berlin, 1860, p. 59. "We heard now why the Christians were imprisoned. They had refused to contribute money towards the superstitious customs which the Chinese observe in times of great droughts; they then pray to the *dragon of the rain* for wet weather. .... On each house pieces of paper are fixed containing prayers, and also the likenesses of the *dragon of the rain*. .... Also images of this dragon made of wood or paper are carried in procession. And if it does not rain, the dragon is smashed.

Under the rule of KiaKing there was a great drought. The dragon would not send rain. The emperor banished the poor dragon to the province of Torgot.

But all the mandarins prayed for his return, when at last the emperor ordered him to be brought back."—*Vide* Huc und Gabet, "Wanderungen durch das Chinesische Reich," bearbeitet von Karl Andree, 1867, p. 67.

The ancient Egyptians represented Knuphis, the god of the snakes, holding a jug, out of which a stream of water flows.—*Vide* Schwartz, "Ursprung der Mythologie," p. 61.

In the Old Testament we have also the water and serpent brought into connection. Thus in Amos ix. 3, the Lord says, "And though they be hid from my sight in the bottom of the sea, *thence will I command the serpent.*" A similar idea to that expressed in the quotation from Strabo is contained in the words of Ezekiel xxix. 3: "I am against thee, Pharaoh, King of Egypt, the great dragon that lieth in the midst of his rivers, which hath said, *My river is mine own and I have made it for myself.*" Also Ezekiel xxxii. 2, in the prophecy against the same king: "Thou art as a *whale in the seas; and thou camest forth with thy rivers.*" And in Isaiah xxvii. 1, we read: "And he shall slay *the dragon that is in the sea.*"

[54] In Germany there is a belief that at the birth of every child a new star appears in the sky. If a person dies, his star falls down from the sky to the earth. Among the Indians of California the Pleiades are said to be women who went to heaven. The aborigines of Peru believed that every animal had a representative amongst the stars. The Yurucares-Indians believed the same.—Bastian, *Zeitschrift für Ethnologie*, 1872, p. 357. The Kirghiz also transfer their deceased to the stars, from where, if invoked, they can come to the earth.—Bastian, "Beiträge zur vergleichenden Psychologie," 1868, p. 89. The Caribs of the West India Islands saw their immortal heroes in the constellations of the stars.—Peschel, "Races of Man," p. 261.

But even if we had not these proofs of a future life

among the Khoikhoi, we should come to the conclusion of the existence of such a belief, from the custom that they bury their dead with the face towards the east. To them also our "Ex oriente lux" had a deeper meaning. Peschel, in his "Races of Man," p. 259, correctly remarks: "Again, if we knew no further details as to the opinions of the intellectually gifted Hottentots, formerly so greatly underrated, it would be enough that, previous to burial, they place the body of the deceased in the same position which it once occupied as an embryo in the mother's womb. The meaning of this significant custom is, that the dead will mature in the darkness of the earth in preparation for a new birth." The graves are covered with stoneheaps and branches of thorns to prevent the hyenas devouring the bodies.

That the pre-historic myth-makers thought very much about the riddle of a future life, we have seen in the myth of the Moon, who sent the Hare to men with the message of immortality.

This feeling of a future life is not as dim as some ethnologists and travellers and missionaries like to represent it. I shall refer to what I experienced myself.

Once I met on the outskirts of the Kalihari a party of Namaquas in an ox waggon, which belonged to a woman of rank (Geikhois), who was with the party. I knew her very well, for she had treated me very hospitably when I once stayed at her kraal. I was very much surprised to find her so far away from her home, and asked: "What brings you into these waterless hunting grounds; since when are women going to shoot game?"

"My dear friend," she said, "don't make fun, I am in great distress; we lost a great number of sheep and cattle through the drought and the Bushmen, and I am going to the grave of my father, who died in the hunting fields; I am going to pray and weep there; he will hear my voice, and he will see my tears, and he will give luck to my husband who is now out ostrich-hunting, so that we can buy again milk-goats and cows, that our little ones may live."

"But your father is dead'" I said; "how will he hear?"

"Yes, he is dead," she answered, "but he only sleeps! We Khoikhoi always, if we are in trouble, go and pray at the graves of our grand-parents and ancestors; it is an old custom of ours."

Is there a difference between this woman and Napoleon III., who, like the old kings of France, was so eager to play the part of the Eldest Son of the Church, and who was certainly addicted to ancestor worship, if the recently published will of April 14th, 1875, is genuine? "We must remember," writes the Emperor, "that those we love look down upon us from Heaven and protect us. It is the soul of my great uncle which has always guided and supported me. Thus will it be with my son, also if he proves worthy of his name."—(*Allgemeine Zeitung*, 1875); *Vide* Peschel, "Races of Man," p. 261.)

Another custom, which also proves that the Khoikhoi believe that the person in the grave is not quite dead, is that of throwing water on the grave shortly after the burial. When asked why they do this, they say, in order to cool the soul of the deceased. The grave is also called ǁaus—*i.e.*, "the unhappy, discontented;" ǁau signifies "dissatisfied." If, for instance, an ox is slaughtered, the cattle can be seen to hold a gathering at that spot, throwing up dust with their horns and feet, and the bulls especially commence roaring like lions. Then the Khoihoi say: Goman ta ǁau, the cattle are dissatisfied—*i.e.*, they protest against the death of their comrade. Another word is ǁauäm, which also means, to protest, but in a very energetic way.

CHAPTER III.

> *I shall indeed interpret all that I can. But I cannot interpret all that I should like.*—GRIMM.

COMMENTARY TO THE PREVIOUS CHAPTER, AND ANALYSIS OF THE MYTHOLOGICAL NAMES.

I HAVE endeavoured to give a collection of the fragments of a very old mythology, in which are contained the remnants of a primæval religion. I am sure that a good number of my readers are disappointed because they missed that high flight of ideas, and that beautiful but deceptive charm which poetry adds to the mythology of the Aryan, and even to that of the Polynesian races. As I said in the first chapter, this collection will be considered very insipid and tasteless, and I shall not be surprised if some will find fault with me for not employing my time in researches concerning a worthier object. I am fully aware of such objections; nay, I hear similar expressions daily; but the more I hear, the more I am alive to the difficulty of my task.

I do not reproach those who, comparing these myths with our Indo-Aryan mythologies, find them very insipid. My readers are Aryans, they belong to that race of mankind which in science, arts, and religion will for ever serve as a standard to all other races on the surface of the earth.

The characteristic of true science always has been to draw objects of the most simple nature and the most simple organization under its microscope, in order to discover the origin of the object, and the mutual connection and reciprocal working of the various powers in Nature.

If we look at the present standard of zoology and biology, it was the study of the most simple organisms which led to results which the wildest imagination of our greatest philosophers never could have dreamt of. The theory of evolution has become an established fact, and there is no science, at present, which could deny its invigorating and propelling power on all the other sciences, and on itself. A short glance at the controversial literature on Darwinism—a literature which, by itself, is sufficient to fill a magnificent library—shows that the cudgels were taken up *pro* and *contra*, by the very best men on both sides; but after a hard and severe contest, the theory of evolution carried the day. If our anatomists and zoologists would have been satisfied with the investigation of the structure and organization of the most developed animals only, they never would have arrived at such astonishing facts, whose full importance is beyond human conception, and only can be dimly guessed.

The same with the science of comparative mythology, and its mother, comparative philology. What has been achieved by this science for the knowledge of the condition of our pre-historic races, we admire in the works of Wilhelm von Humboldt, Bopp, Pott, von der Gabelentz, Kuhn, Grimm, Schwartz, and Max Müller. But all those men had chiefly as their object of investigation the Aryan races; very little or nothing, comparatively, has been done in the realm of the languages of the Great Dark Continent, with the exception of the Hamitic languages. The science of language and the science of religion are, as regards South Africa, entirely in an embryonic state. Pott and von der Gabelentz, famous through their discoveries in the Aryan realm, were the first to draw an outline ¹sketch of the Kafir-Congo, or so-called Bantu languages; and a few years before them, Norris, in Prichard's "Natural

History of Man," was the one to analyse the Khoikhoi idioms, and to show them their place among the tongues of the world.

Then followed the late Dr. Bleek, who succumbed under the gigantic work he had begun to give to us, after the model of Bopp, a comparative grammar of the South African languages. Bishop Callaway has commenced to collect materials for the foundation of a comparative mythology of the South African races, but nothing of any importance has been done since. The fact of the matter is, that there is a great lack of that truly scientific idealism, which will, uninfluenced by public opinion and newspaper criticism, pursue its course with an indomitable spirit, fully convinced that it is done in the service of the elevation of mankind. There is no Chair as yet for Comparative Ethnology and the Science of Language in our colleges, where the younger generations could be made acquainted with the natural and mental condition of the aborigines. Our native policy will remain a fruitless experiment as long as we do not know our coloured brethren. And the great stumbling-block to carry out a fruitful native policy is the mutual hatred between the Europeans and aborigines. There is such a hatred, and it is dangerously increasing. Who can deny that nine-tenths of the white population of South Africa look down upon the aborigines as a superior kind of the baboon tribe. And still we pretend to be good Christians, and call ourselves "Christenmenschen." We do not see how paradoxical and pharisaical we are. If we only knew more about the way of thinking of the natives, if we only could imagine that there is in those black bodies a religious sentiment which craves for a sight of the Unknown, as our own heart yearns for the Invisible, we would soon drop our self-conceit.

This ill feeling can only be removed if Ethnology and Comparative Philology will form one of the subjects in our code of higher education, and I should think that, after twenty years, the stumbling-block in the progress of civilization in our colonies will be removed. Only a sound study and an unprejudiced knowledge of the native mind will qualify us to produce a sound and safe native policy.

We will learn to appreciate in the native what is good, and be anxious to bring the good qualities to a harmonious development. For his faults and vices our education and training will supply the necessary remedy. This would be the practical value of the study of Ethnology, under which heading I comprise the theoretical study of the South African languages, for the purpose of learning the prehistoric condition of the Aborigines, and their present natural condition, customs, manners, and religion.

When Bopp, Pott, and Grimm laid the foundation-stone of that glorious work, the Comparative Grammar and Comparative Mythology of the Aryan races, we should not forget that more than twenty centuries had contributed towards the bricks and mortar and tools with which that magnificent temple was erected. And here, in South Africa, what have we to boast of? Since Sir George Grey left our shores, and Dr. Bleek is not more amongst us, it almost seems that the work, so energetically commenced, is going to collapse. We cannot yet think of constructing such an edifice, which could stand a comparison with that grand temple erected by Bopp, before all the materials are prepared and their collection is secured. Our task, and that of the next generation, is to collect every possible and reliable material; and what already is collected should be thrown on the market, to be moulded and shaped into bricks. The linguistic and ethnological world, both of Europe and America, daily ask, *Quid novi ex Africa?* The foundation-stone is well laid, but where are the languages, the myths, and legends of those nations, of whom we had some dim idea, and whose existence has been confirmed by the discoveries of Cameron and Stanley? And in the most southern part of our continent—that is, British South Africa, a vast territory bordering in the north on the banks of the Kunene and Zambesi rivers—there lives a most unique race, represented in two peculiar branches of the Hottentot race, by the Khoikhoi and Bushman family. What may I ask, has been done to secure the necessary materials for a comparative study of their languages, mythologies, customs and manners? There are sundry translations of parts and extracts of the Bible, but more or less in one and the same Khoikhoi dialect. Twelve dialects, spoken in Great Namaqualand, are still unrecorded. The little we know of the |Kora, which bears the most ancient type of the Khoikhoi, like Sanscrit among the Indo-European languages, is very insufficiently known, and this tribe is now on the point of dying out. Of the old Colonial Khoikhoi, the so-called Cape Hottentot, we know little or nothing. The few words recorded by Witsen, Ten Rhyne, Hervas, Kolb, Valentyn, Leibniz, Spaarmann, Thunberg, Barrow, Liechtenstein, and Le Vaillant, and few others, are written in such unintelligible and distorted orthography that they are useless for comparative purpose. Even the student who is well acquainted with a Hottentot dialect is hardly able to use these specimens with any success.

Four years ago a man of the tribe, to whom the Moravian missionary, George Schmidt, brought the Gospel, died at Bredasdrop; eight months ago, another old Cape Khoikhoi died at Moddergat, Stellenbosch district; another last year close to the Paarl; and six years ago one in Cape Town, who all spoke their old language.

The late Dr. Bleek therefore was misinformed when he stated that the old Cape type had entirely died out. There are at this moment some alive, *and it is of vital importance that our Government should grant* a small sum for the purpose of searching for such individuals, and collecting from their lips these long-forgotten dialects.

I said ethnology should be taught at our colleges, and I have also pointed out the practical result it would have for a sound and just native policy. If this could be done, and a warm enthusiastic interest for these studies be instilled into our rising generation, the eyes of the scientific world would look with admiration towards the Cape.

But our students must be taught, "what to observe, and how to observe." To draw the public interest towards these studies we require an ethnological museum, after the model of the ethnological museums in Berlin, Leipsic, and London. What we possess in this respect at the Cape is not beyond the appearance of a curiosity shop. But before we can expect valuable contributions towards such an institution, we must have men who understand the importance of this science; such men, however, we must educate up to the mark. And have we not got in Cape Town, close at hand, all that we could wish for? There is the Breakwater Convict Station, with natives from almost every tribe in South Africa. There are at present chiefs from whose lips valuable information of the history of their tribes and wanderings could be collected; of the customs, of the manners, and of the laws of inheritance and relationship. Instead of that, we are treated by newspaper writers with fruitless controversies about our right to locking up savage tyrants and allowing them a smaller number of wives than they had been accustomed to. Is there a place in the whole of South Africa where, with so little expense, anatomical measurements and studies for anthropological purposes could be carried on?—results for which our Darwins, Huxleys, Haeckels, Weissbachs, Vogts, Fritschs, and other anthropologists beg and crave; and still, it seems, there is no ear to hear them! Is there a better opportunity for our Cape Colleges to demonstrate anthropology, *ad oculos*, than at the Breakwater?—where the method of anatomical measurement could be taught with greater success?

And if the Cape Government has no eye and ear, or no means for the establishment of such an anthropological institute, is there no influential *savant* who would raise his voice to induce the various Governments of the civilized world to co-operate in founding an "International Anthropological Institute at the Cape of Good Hope?"

Most of our young college students become public men. They enter the civil service; some become field-cornets, judges of the peace, members of Parliament, and magistrates or magistrate's clerks; others, again, farmers and merchants. Every one almost will come in contact with natives. Our college students come from every part of South Africa. Does it not lie in the power of our Government, in connection with the Educational Board and the Philosophical Society, to organize and to encourage the collecting of linguistic and mythological materials, which materials should be published under the superintendence and editorship of an enthusiastic and competent scholar? In this way only should we be able to supply the scientific market in Europe, where hundreds of hands stand ready to coin the ore thus produced. This would not only give to all comparative sciences—especially to comparative psychology (*Völkerpsychologie*)—a new stimulus, but it would be the most expedient and cheapest way of furthering the progress of comparative sciences in our country.

The fragments recorded in the preceding chapter are, if we read them without a commentary, on the whole not very poetical—nay, some are of a repulsive character. As soon, however, as we put them under the microscope of the etymologist, we shall find that these myths are not more meaningless than the germs of those mythologies which have filled with deep devotional feelings the hearts of our own Aryan ancestors, before they migrated to the South, North, East and West.

But to come to a clear understanding the reader

should be careful not to mix up terms of such essential difference as religion and mythology. Many an educated man we hear expressing the idea that mythology and religion, as far as heathens and savages are concerned, are synonymous. They seem not to know that *there is only one religion commou to all mortals*, and that this religion is based on faith. Mythology, however, is a secondary element in the history of the development of the human mind ; wherever religion crops up, mythology will serve as a cloak to disguise her true beautiful form ; and in the same way as the cloak sometimes adopts the form of a statue, or of the human body, in the same way mythology often copies in a bewildering manner from religion.

If we want to understand the original meaning of a myth, we have to trace it back to its fountain. We have to study the history of the names of the persons who act a part in a mythological tale back to its origin, by stripping off all garments, which time and every new generation have added to it, until we arrive at the naked root and original meaning of the word. The comparative philologist, in a certain sense of the word, works like the Bushman, who, with a keen eye, well acquainted with the habits and—may I use the expression—the way of thinking of the game, follows on their track and examines every pebble turned in their hasty flight. Sometimes the footprints are very clear, where the soil is very soft. Sometimes they disappear altogether on rocky ground ; and here it is where the hunter has to call in his practical knowledge of the nature of the game and the topographical condition of the country. So the mythologist with the honest endeavour to feel and think like a primæval man, with an almost childlike way of expressing himself, and at the same time well trained in the method and practice of comparative philology, has to follow up the history of a mythological name, until he arrives at the true meaning of it. He always must bear in mind "*that language is always language—it always meant something originally,"* and *"that it is the essential character of a true myth, that it should be no longer intelligible."*—Max Müller.

"The facts of language, however small, are historical facts, and require an historical explanation." Therefore, I shall try in the sequel of this chapter to give for each mythological name a rational and etymological explanation, inasmuch as I do not care to have these myths considered a conglomerate of meaningless and insipid tales.

In the growth and change of the Khoikhoi mythology we find an analogy to the growth and change of mythology among the Aryan nations. Amongst the Khoikhoi also, as amongst the Aryans, there was a "tendency to change the original conceptions of divine powers, to misunderstand the many names given to those powers, and even to misinterpret the praises given to them. In this manner some of the divine names were changed into the half-divine." [2]

Tsũi‖goab.

I shall begin with that name which calls forth even to-day the deepest feelings of devotion and reverence in the heart of a Khoikhoi. *Tsũi‖goab*, originally *Tsuni‖goam*, was the name by which the [3]Redmen called the Infinite. Modern translators and interpreters, such as serve on mission stations, generally explain it, "*Sore or wounded knee,*" from *tsū* or *tsũi*, wounded, sore, and ‖goab or ‖khoab, the knee. And I myself, some ten years ago, have in a controversial paper,[4] "Der Hottentotische Tsũi‖goab und der Griechische Zeus," been in favour of this explanation. After a more careful study of the matter, however, I have now good reason to discard my former opinion, and to replace it, as I hope, by a more reasonable explanation, based on the method of sound etymological investigation. For if the former translation were correct, and if this name by which the Infinite is invoked were so transparent as to demand such an interpretation, Tsũi‖goab could not be a mythological being, but simply a person who acts a part in some common fable. Let us therefore try a new analysis.

The word is composed of two independent roots, *tsu* and ‖*goa*. ‖*Goa* means to walk, to go on, to approach, to march on, to come on. Now in Khoikhoi it is exactly the same whether I say, *mu-b* or *mu-m*, seeing-he, he-sees, or *mu-b*, *mu-m*, the-eye—*i.e.*, the-seer, the-seeing-one. The same, there is no difference whether I say, ‖*goa-b*, ‖*goa-m*, coming-he, approaching-he—*i.e.*, he comes, he approaches —or whether I say, ‖*goa-b*, ‖*goa-m*, the-approaching-one—viz., day, or the morning, the dawn; or if I say, ‖*goa-b*, ‖*goa-m*, the-going-one, the-walking-one—*i.e.*, the knee.

We have in Khoikhoi the following words :—‖*Goa-b*, the morning, the daybreak; ‖*goa-b*, the knee; ‖*goara*, the day dawns, it dawns, it is dawning. Metaphorically ‖*goa* means also "*to pray,*" because it is an old Khoikhoi custom to go out away from the house as soon as the first beams of the dawn shoot up in the East, and to kneel behind a bush to pray. The original " ‖*goatara*, ǀ*gore ta niga*," " I go out to pray" (ǀgore or ǀgure, to pray), has dwindled down into " ‖*goatara*"—*i.e.*, " I go," *I pray*, just as our " *I wish you a good morning*," has collapsed into " *Good morning*," and even " *Morning.*"

It is now obvious that ǁ*goab* in *Tsũi*‖*goab* cannot be translated with *knee*, but we have to adopt the other metaphorical meaning, *the approaching* day—*i.e.*, the dawn.

We come now to the root *Tsũ*. It meant originally " what is sore, what is wounded, what is hurt, what is painful." Derivative forms were *tsuni*, *tsũi*, and *tsũ*. Now, among the Nama-tribe generally, *tsũ* and *tsũi*, mean " sore, wounded, hurt, affected with a wound, or with pain; while *tsũ*, a more dilapidated form of *tsuni*, has a metaphorical meaning, "unpleasant, difficult, troublesome, painful." This, however, is not the case in all Nama dialects; sometimes the two words are promiscuously pronounced and applied. From this tsŭ, by reduplication, is formed a verb, tsŭ-tsŭ, to hurt a person, and ‡nou-tsŭ-tsŭ, to hurt a person by beating, or, as we say, *to beat a person black and blue.*

The colour of a wound is *red*, especially of a fresh wound received in a battle, and thus *tsu* can signify *red*, just as |ava or |aua, "red," meant originally *bloody*, blood-coloured (|au-b, *blood*). *Tsu*||*goab* or *Tsûi*||*goab* therefore, verbally translated, is *the-red-morning, the-red-daybreak*—*i.e.*, the *dawn*.

This etymology is strengthened by the following circumstances:—First, I have said in the second chapter that the |Koras believe *Tsûi*||*goam* to live in the Red-Heaven or Red-Sky. Then, in the next pages will be proved that ‡*Ei*χ*a*|*kha*||*nabiseb* and *Tsûi*||*goab* are identical, and in the Hymn of ‡*Ei*χ*a*|*kha*||*nabiseb* is said of him, "*thou* who painteth thyself with *red ochre.*" And, third, when the *day dawns* the Khoikhoi go and pray, with the face turned towards the East: "Oh, Tsu||goa, All-Father." We are also told that the Khoikhoi, especially their women, paint themselves with red ochre, if they offer prayers at the cairns of Heitsi-eibib (Dapper, Witsen).

Here, as it often happens in mythology, as well as in our daily life, a person is often called after the abode or place he inhabits. We have in our Colony names as *van Breda, van Gent*, &c., meaning originally certainly nothing else, but *the man of Breda, the man of Gent.* In the same manner the ancient Khoikhoi in their yearning after the Infinite transferred the name of his supposed abode upon Him who thrones on high. Hence the origin of the name *Tsûi*||*goab* for the Supreme Being.

The myth now tells us that *Tsûi*||*goab* is the avenger of men, and that he kills ||Gaunab, the evil-doer. He also can see what is going to happen in future; he is a seer, a prophet. In the Vedic mythology Saranyu, the Dawn, is also the avenger, and can also predict what will happen. The Germans have still the proverbial saying:—

>Es ist nichts so fein gesponnen,
>Es kommt doch endlich an der Sonnen.
>(Nothing is so finely spun,
>It must come before the sun.)

The Sanskrit *Saranyu* or *Dyaus* has etymologically certainly nothing to do with the Khoikhoi *Tsũi‖goab*, and certainly the one is not derived from the other. And still, in a certain sense, *Dyaus* or *Saranyu*, and *Tsũi‖goab* stand in very close connection, according to the maxim that the human mind all over the world is the same, and consequently will use certain striking phenomena in Nature as a base for the same figure of speech.

Other names for the Infinite among the Khoikhoi are ǀ*Khūb, Tusib,* ǀ*Nanub* ǀ*Gurub, Heitsi-eibib,* ‖*Khāb,* ‡*Ei*χa-ǀ*kha*‖*nabiseb,* and ǀ*Gurikhoisib.* Of these we shall treat hereafter. As *Tsũi-‖goab* is always mentioned in connection with his opponent, or better with the demon ‖*Gaunab,* we shall have at first to deal with him, and to analyze his name, and then we shall see how mythology set to work, generation after generation, until it produced the legend with the variations recorded in the preceding chapter.

‖*Gaunam.*

If the name of Tsũi-‖goab only fills the mind of a Khoikhoi with joy, gratitude, and veneration, the name of ‖*Gaunab* always confers to him the idea of pain, misery, and death. The root ‖Gau means to destroy, to annihilate, to mangle; from this we have the derivative ‖gaurà, bad, spoiled, worthless, infected; ‖gaub, destruction, ruination, annihilation; hence ‖*Gaunab,* the destroyer, the one who annihilates.

Who was now, according to the idea of the ancient Khoikhoi, the destroyer? Certainly nobody else but the night, *Tsuχub*. We have the root ||ō, and from this the following derivatives: —||ō, to die; ||ōm, to sleep; ||ō-b, death, illness, disease, ||om-s, sleep, ||oreb, guilt, sin, what is liable to death, crime; ||oreχa, wicked, sinful, guilty, criminal. Now, the night makes the people fall 'asleep or to die (||ō ||om), to be in a death-like state. The Khoikhoi say that ||Gaunab lives in the black heaven or black sky. The night sky, however, is the black sky. Consequently the black sky, at whose approach men ||o, die, or ||om, *sleep*, is the night sky—that is, ||*Gaunab*, the destroyer.

It will now be obvious that originally the words ||*Gauna* and *Tsũi*||*goa* were intended for nothing else than to illustrate metaphorically the change of day and night. Then the words Tsũi||goa and ||Gauna came down to the following generations, whilst their original meaning was lost. Mythology and religious sentiment stepped in at once and set to work. There was the belief of a power which sends its blessings to the earth to benefit men. Man died every evening, and the dark night covered him; the approaching dawn opened his eyes to new life, he felt refreshed. He turned his eyes towards the East, and saw the sky red, blood-red, sore like a fresh battle-wound. Blood had been spilled, a battle had taken place; so he fancied in his simple puerile way of thinking; and as he came to life with the dawn, what was more natural than that his mythological instinct invented the story of a battle between ||*Gaunab*, who lives in the black sky, and Tsũi ||goab, who lives in the red sky, in the dawn? Tsũi||goab was now a hero, who had received a *wound at his knee*. The rosy dawn was exchanged for a lame, broken knee.

Every tribe, every clan, every family, naturally has an ancestor, and if his name is lost, the myth-forming power very soon will invent one. Such ancestor, naturally enough, is a hero, who does wonderful things.

Tsūi-ǁgoab, the giver of all blessings, *the Father on high*, *All-Father*, the avenger, who fought daily the battle for his people, thus was identified with the ancestor of the tribe whose name was forgotten. Hence we have the ancestor-worship growing together with the worship of the Infinite —that is, *vice versâ*, *Tsūiǁgoab*, the dawn, became the mythical ancestor of the Khoikhoi.

Each tribe afterwards ascribed to this hero such qualities as were peculiar to, and popular among, themselves. And as there are other powers in Nature which also bestow blessings on men, like the rain, the thunderstorm, the moon, the wind (especially the rain, wind, the sun, the clouds), and as these powers also have been personified, it was only quite natural that they are either identified with the Supreme Being, or that they are considered as emanations or relations of his. Therefore it is that this Being must have a wife, ǀUrisis; a son, ǀUrisib, like every human father, grandfather, and hero. Hence we find, not only among the Khoikhoi, but among all other, especially the higher, mythologies, a real Olympian genealogy.

ǀKhub.

Tsūiǁgoab is also called ǀKhūb. This is the general term with which a chief, a ruler, a rich man, a master, is addressed. If *Tsūiǁgoab* is the father and ruler of the Khoikhoi he must be rich (ǀKhū) and powerful. ǀKhūb signifies the Lord, and is derived from the root ǀKhū, to be laden with something. A pregnant woman is a ǀkhūi or ǀkhuni taras—*i.e.*, a laden, a burdened woman. A rich man has always been an influential man, a ruling man; hence it is that ǀKhū has adopted the meaning to rule, to be a lord. *Tariëǁnaba ra ǀkhū?* (who is king there? or, who rules there?) has become identical with *Tarie ǁnaba ra gao-ao?* (*gao-ao-b*, king, chief).

This brings us to the next point, to show how, in the

capacity as |Khūb, Tsūi|goab is identical with |Nanub, the thunder-cloud, and |Gurub, the thunder.

|Nanub.

|Nanub is in Khoikhoi the *thunder-cloud*, and shows the root |na, *to filter, to stream*. It means especially that kind of streaming which a man can observe if he digs for water in the sand of a periodical river. That filtering and streaming together of the water from various sides is |nā. Therefore, |Nanub is the filterer, the pourer, or, to speak in South African Dutch, "'de Zuiverwater," an expression which well applies to the nature of the rain-pouring cloud.

|Gurub.

|Gurub, on first sight, makes the impression of being an onomatopoeticon, imitating the sound of the thunder; but this is only a delusion. The root of |gurub is |gū, which means to cover, to envelop (in German, umhüllen, verhüllen, bedecken). The following will plainly show what the Khoikhoi understand by the word |gū. I once had bought ostrich eggs, some of which were already on the point of breaking open and producing chickens. I did not like to destroy the rest, and asked the Namaqua who had given them to me how to hatch them, when he said: |Giri- ǂnams |khats ni |gūte (You must *cover* them with a jackal caross). Also the skin or cloak which the women wear round the lower body for the purpose of covering it, is called ʼ|gubib, *the coverer*. From this, |gu again, two mountains in Great Namaqualand are called *Geitsi-*|*gubib* (Great |Gubib), and ǂKharisi-|gubis (Little |Gubis). The Geitsi |gubib is a crater-shaped mountain, without being of volcanic origin. |Gurub therefore means the coverer, and was one of the names of the thunder-cloud |Nanub, which covers the sky. A savage believes, that if it thunders, somebody is speaking out of the cloud, or the cloud itself is speaking.

In the same way as the Infinite was called the Dawn, Tsũi‖goab, now the Thunder, in the same manner, accepted the name of the thunder-cloud, for his abode, and hence he was called ǃGurub. In the Rigveda the cloud is also called vritra—*i.e.*, the coverer—and Vritra is also the name of the demon slain by Indra. Here, quite independently from the Khoikhoi, the ancient worshippers of Dyaus have developed almost the same idea. In the Rigveda, it says, that Indra with the Maruts (winds) fights Vritra, who keeps the sunlight from the earth. — (*Vide* Benfey, " Sanskrit Dictionary," p. 895 ; and Schwartz, " Ursprung der Mythologie," pp. 50, 95, 132.)

One often hears the following sayings among the Namaquas :—ǀ*Nanub ga* ǀ*guruo, ob ge geise ni* ǁǀ*na*—that is, if the cloud is *covering* (rising from the horizon, and towering one above the other towards the zenith), then it will pour down very much. And again : ǀNanub ga ǀhomgu ei ǁgoeö, on ge khoina, ǀnanub ge ǀhomga ra ǀgū-ǂgã (or ǀguruǂgã), tira mi. If the thunder-cloud lies on the mountains, then the people say the clouds *envelop* the mountains. And again: ǀAvi-ǁaib ǀnati ge ǀkhunusete ǀnanubi ra ǀguru-ǂgãhe. In the rainy season the Pleiades are enveloped by the thunder-cloud. All these sayings clearly show the true meaning of ǀGurub, that it originally meant the *coverer ;* and only in the course of time, when this first meaning was forgotten and lost, by the agency of the myth-forming power, it assumed the meaning, the *thunderer.* That there is still a recollection of the first meaning is quite certain. An old Namaqua said to me once, after a heavy thunderstorm had passed over the country : " ǀGurub ke geise ko ǀavi," meaning, " the thunder-cloud has rained very hard."

Here the original meaning crops up again. For ǀ*Gurub ra* ǀ*avi* is generally said, ǀ*Nanub ke ra* ǀ*avi,* or ǀ*Nanub ke ra tū,* the cloud is raining. The cloud, ǀ*Nanub,* is often implored thus:

ǀNanutseǃ

Sida ǃKhutseǃ
ǀAvire or ǀavi geire!
(Oh Cloud, our Lord, let rain, or simply, rain then!)
And in the preceding chapter, ǃGurub is called, in a hymn, ǀNanumatse, thou son of the cloud. Consequently there is no doubt left as to ǀNanub and ǃGurub.

Identity of Tsũiǁgoab and ǃGurub and ǀNanub.

It is not necessary now to enter into any further analysis in order to identify ǀNanub and ǃGurub with Tsũiǁgoab, lest we should become very tedious in our explanations. I will briefly point out the most essential parts of comparison and similarity. Tsũiǁgoab, ǀNanub, and ǃGurub, are all in the same manner implored, "*let rain.*" ǃGurub especially is addressed, "*not to speak too angrily to men;*" who else, then, can he be than the All-Father, Tsũiǁgoab, who scolds his children? Valentyn, as we saw in the second chapter, also quotes both names for the same god, *Tuiqua* (*Tsũiǁgoab*), and *Gourrou* (*ǃGurub*). Leibniz ("Collectanea Etymologica," Hannover, 1717, p. 377), always uses the name *Thoro*, for God, which is nothing else than ǃGuru; t' generally being applied by those ancient travellers and writers to express the click, or a click with g, h, k.

ǁKhāb, Heitsi-eibib, ǀGarubeb and Tusib.

ǁ*Khāb*, originally ǁKhami, still in ǀKora, ǁKhām, is derived from the root ǁ*Khā, the same, again;* for instance, the pronoun ǁkhāb, the same, and words like ǁkhaba or ǁkhava, again, in return; ǁkhara, to punish, to revenge—that is, to do to a person the same that he has done to others; ǁkharas, punishment, retaliation; ǁkhai, to turn, to bring back—for instance, ǁkhai gomaba, turn the ox; ǁkha-ǁkha, to teach, to train—*i.e.*, to turn over and over again, to turn a person again and again, until he learns to go the straight course; all these derivatives come from the radix, ǁKha. As I pointed out some pages back, there is no difference in Khoikhoi if I say mũ-b, he-sees, or ªmũb, the eye—*i.e.*, the seer—and ǁgoa-b, he walks, or

‖goa-b, the knee—*i.e.*, the walker; in the same way there is no difference if we say ³‖Kha-mi, ‖Kha-m, or ‖Khă-b, he-is-returning, or the return-er—that is, the moon. When after a few dark nights the silver crescent of the moon appeared again on the western horizon, the ancient Khoikhoi would say, "*Ah, there he is again.*" And when, in the course of time, the pronoun of the third person had also accepted the office of a sex-denoting classifier or article, then the predicative, ‖Kha-m or ‖Khă-b, he-returns, he-is-there-again, became the appellative, ‖Khăb, or ‖Khām, the returner *par excellence*. When even this meaning was lost, the next generation beheld ‖Khăb as a *nomen proprium* of the moon.

The resemblances between ‖Khām, the Moon, and Tsūi‖goam, the Dawn, are very striking. We said in the second chapter that the moon promises immortality to men, and when they were deceived by the hare, he is also the avenger, punishing the latter. Tsūi‖goab every morning gives life to men, and from the battle with ‖Gaunam he received a wound; also the hare scratches the moon's face. Of Tsūi‖goab it is also said, like the moon, that he often dies and rises again. He (Tsūi‖goab) being a person of supernatural powers can take all kinds of shapes, he also can disappear, or become suddenly invisible. It is the same again with the moon, who assumes different shapes, and sometimes disappears altogether. The disappearing of the moon is called ‖ō, to die; on the dying or disappearing of the moon, especially if there be an eclipse of the moon, great anxiety prevails. One would almost believe that a great calamity has befallen a kraal, such is the disturbance on such occasions. I have seen the people moaning and crying as though suffering great pain. Those prepared for a hunting expedition, or already hunting in the field, will immediately return home, and postpone their undertakings. Does it not sound to us as if we hear the old Psalmist praying :—

Have mercy upon me, O God—
Cast me not away from thy presence;
Restore unto me the joy of thy salvation!

That the Moon is identical with Tsũi‖goab, as the "Lord of Light and Life," can, after these explanations, be no longer doubtful. And it is also obvious from the antiquated and obliterated nature of the name itself, that the Moon was already worshipped as *the Visible God* of the Khoikhoi before their separation.

We come now to Heitsi-eibib. As to him, the etymology of his name offers considerable difficulty. Generally, interpreters translate it "prophet," "foreteller," "the one who can predict what will happen." And this translation or etymology is based on cutting Heitsi-eibib up into two words—*Heisi*, to tell, to give a message, to order; and *eibe*, before, beforehand, previously. Consequently Heitsi-eibib would mean the foreteller, the prophet. Here, again, as we remarked in the analysis of Tsũi‖goab, if the word Heitsi-eibib is so transparent as to be so easily explained, the whole mythology in regard to him would collapse into a meaningless and insipid fable. We therefore must look for a more satisfactory and rational explanation.

To the linguist it will be quite clear that only two roots, *hei* and *ei*, are contained in the word *Hei-tsi-ei-bi-b*; all the other syllables are suffixes. *Hei* means everything that belongs to the *wood or shrub line*, anything that has a wooden nature. We have thus hei-b, a pole, a stick, a staff, a collection of trees (German, *Gebüsch*); hei-s, fem., a tree, and hei-ï, a tree in general, a piece of wood, or a shrub. From this *hei* we have derivatives like *hei-χa*, rich in wood, full of shrubs, full of trees; heitsi or heisi, wood-like, having the appearance of a tree, (as adjective derivative), and heirab, the juice of the mimosa tree (gum arabic). But there is also a verbal derivative, *hei-sī*, to send a stick (from hei, stick, and sī, to send)—that is, to order, to send a message. This *sī*, to send, must not be mixed up with si, suffix pronominal and suffix adjective, which is identical with our *ly*. With *si*, to send, the following compounds are formed:—*Asi*, to cause to drink; asi gomana, bring the cattle to the water, let the cattle drink; daisi, to nurse, *i.e.*, to cause the child to drink, to put the child to the breast. Thus, to come back to *heisī*, it signifies, originally, to send a stick, a staff, and then, to send a message, to order. Chiefs, if they send a man with a summons to another person, give the messenger, as a credential, their staff, the emblem of their power; hence the name heisi-aob, the staff-bearing man—*i.e.*, the messenger. The man summoned is simply touched with the staff and he has to follow immediately. Here, however, we have not to do with the verbal derivative *hei-si*, to order, but with the adjective derivative heisi or heitsi, wooden, wood-like, having a tree-like appearance. For we have the form Hei*tsi*-eibib, and not Heisi-eibib. Only the adjective suffix °*tsi* can change into *si*, and *vice versâ*, but the verbal form *si*, to send, could never change into *tsi*. Thus, we have Gei*tsi*|gubib (masc. sing.), name of a mountain, and ‡Khari*si*|gubis (fem. sing.), also a name of a mountain; ||gū*tsi*||gubib (masc. sing.), the male frog; ||gū*si*||gūbis (fem. sing.), the female frog; sir*tsi*|gūbib (masc. sing.), the male bat; sir*si*|gubis (fem. sing.), the female bat. But *asi*, to cause to drink, or *daisi*, to cause to suck—*i.e.*, to nurse, or *heisi*, to send a message—could never be transformed into *ātsi*, *daitsi*, *heitsi*, maintaining the same meanings as verbs. Therefore *Heitsi* in *Heitsi*-eibib is the adjective derivative suffix for the masculine gender, and the only correct translation therefore is, *tree-like, or similar to a tree.*

The fact also that the other and shorter name of *Heitsi-eibib* is *Heigeib*, Great-Tree (from *hei*, tree, and *gei*, great), forces us to translate *Heitsi* into *tree-like*. In the sequel we shall see that this *Heitsi-eibib* is identical with |*Gurikhoisib*, whose other name is ‡Eiχa|kha||nabiseb. And of this person the Lion, in our second chapter, says : ||Khū|nomab, *Mimosaroot* has killed me. And besides, on the graves of *Heitsi-eibib*, as we have had repeatedly occasion to show, branches of trees, pieces of wood, and flowers are strewn as an offering.

These evidences are strong enough to defend our position against any insinuation in favour of the translation " to send a message."

We have now to analyse the meaning of *eibe* or *eibi*. *Eis* or *eib* means the surface—for instance, |hub-eib, earth's-face, orbis terrarum; *eis* or *eib* also means appearance, likeness; for instance, ||eïb *eiba* ta ho‡ui tama, I do not find out his appearance—*i.e.*, I do not identify him, I do not know him. Then we have the names *See-eis*, |Hom-eib, ‡Khoa-eib, *Aniχa-eibib*, all containing the root *ei*, with the meaning face, appearance, likeness. Consequently the only correct translation of *Heitsi-eibib* is, " the One who has the appearance of a tree," and this tree is the magnificent *Dawn-tree*. When, especially in our latitudes, we look towards the East at daybreak, who, if he has any love for the grandeur of Nature, does not admire those beautiful beams and rays shooting up from a central point like the gigantic branches of a magnificent tree.

The points of comparison between Heitsi-eibib and Tsūi||goab and ||Khāb are here again very striking, and leave no doubt as to their being identical. All three come from the East, and this is why, as already stated, the doors of the huts and the graves are found in that direction. The bodies of the deceased are also placed towards the East, so that their faces may look towards sunrise. Even those who possess waggons place them in such a position, that the front is open to the morning sun. And the Khoikhoi, when asked for the reason why they do so, always answer, " Our grandfather *Tsūi||goab*, or our ancestor *Heitsi-eibib*, came from the East." Both are invoked as " *Father*" or " *All-Father*." Every prayer commences *Sida* ītse, or Abo-ītse. Both are rich and possessed of plenty of cattle and sheep. They all promise immortality to men, and fight with the bad beings; they kill the enemies of their people. All three can alter their shape; they can disappear and reappear.

Heitsie-ibib, however, is full of tricks, and his character is not altogether blameless. The sacred legend accuses him of the same crime as that for which Hippolytus and Œdipus have become famous.

It is impossible to deny that the story of Heitsie-ibib committing rape on his mother, taken in its literal meaning, is very repulsive, and not at all in accordance with the code of morals and decency among the Khoikhoi. The laws and customs of the Namaquas are against incest in any form. In the last thirty years only three cases, and those among the so-called [10] Orlam tribes, have happened. Here, certainly, we have the fact of the contact with civilized races having proved fatal to the morals of the Aborigines. When these cases happened there was throughout Great Namaqualand a general outcry of indignation against the criminals; they were punished most severely, thrown out of society, and a gloom was cast over the whole tribe to which they belonged.

The myth of Heitsi-eibib and his mother is certainly not of a recent date; it could not even have been formed at the time when those abstract words "humanity, purity, truth, faith, self-respect, friendship, love, decency," and many more of those beautiful abstract expressions with which the Khoikhoi abounds, were formed. It is one of the oldest mythological relics brought down to us, like an erratic block, and shows that there was a period, below the first layers of culture, when the feelings of morals and decency among the Hottentots were still a *tohu wabohu*, similar to a period in the primitive history of our own race.

The Namaqua, from whose lips I gathered that legend, told me that when he heard it from his grandfather, the old man was of opinion that the story was a very repulsive one. Such things were not done now. This shows us that the story must be a very old one. But if we take the trouble to divest it of the repulsive crust which language and mythology in their natural decay have formed around it, we shall find this old myth intelligible, and discover a meaning in the most meaningless, and a taste and a flavour in the most insipid.

A few pages back, I identified *Heitsi-eibib* with the moon. If we now transfer this legend from the earth to the sky, we shall soon discover that it is nothing else but an illustration of what passes in the journey of the moon from the first quarter until it is the full moon, and back until it is the last quarter.

At first Heitsi-eibib is a baby, and his mother carries him on her back in the Hottentot fashion. A look at the evening sky, when the crescent disc of the moon appears almost above, or on top of the sun, no doubt gave rise to the idea of a mother carrying her child. He is dirty like a helpless child, and the mother who carries him receives a share of the filth. This we translate into our language: The sun sinks into the hazy horizon, into the banks of mist, her face is no longer clear, it becomes dusk, even small patches of clouds appear before her. Then, when the other people are absent, *Heitsi-eibib* gets big, and throws his mother to the ground, and covers her. In our modern style we should say: Every day the moon grows bigger until we have the full moon; the stars are not to be seen, they are absent in the daylight. At the full moon, when that planet has reached her greatest size, the sun sinks immediately below the horizon, her light disappears, and the glorious light of the moon rules now on earth, where formerly sunlight ruled.

Heitsi-eibib then becomes small again, he resumes his former childlike appearance, his mother does not take notice of him, she throws him aside. This, again, everybody can observe how, from full moon to the last quarter, the moon loses in size, until at last nothing of ǃKhāb is to be seen. His mother, the sun, has thrown him away.

I have, in the preceding pages, also drawn a comparison between *Tsūiǁgoab*, the Dawn, and *Heitsi-eibib*. In Greek mythology we meet with a similar interpretation of the changes produced in Nature by the rising and setting sun. Œdipus marries Jocaste (the Dawn), after he has killed his father Laios (the Night). Still more striking is the similarity of ideas in the myth of Hippolytus and Phædra, when compared with Heitsi-eibib and his mother. Delbrück has most ingeniously endeavoured to prove this legend to be the explanation of the phenomenon we see passing every month in the sky, between moon and sun.

The Khasias in North-western India have also brought sun and moon into connection, accusing him of being inflamed with love for his step-mother, the sun, who throws ashes in his face. And for this very reason it is that we see the spots in the moon.

The Esquimo also accord to the moon an unnatural love for his sister the sun, who smears some mud over his face to frighten him away.

On the Isthmus of Darien we also meet with the superstition that the so-called man in the moon is guilty of incest with his sister.

The various ideas which different nations have entertained about the moon, and also about the so-called man in the moon, are very curious. It is impossible to give here a survey of all the superstitions and legends of this kind. The most interesting may, however, here find a place. It is very peculiar that the moon and the hare are brought into connection in various parts of the world. Besides the Khoikhoi, the Herero, a Bantu nation in South-west Africa, have a superstition, that, if it is the last quarter of the moon, Omueze uanos' ombi—that is, the moon—has burnt the hare (Hahn, "Hererogrammatik," p. 155). In Germany

(Westfalia, Soester Börde) the country people say, that if a hare screams in the daytime, he is asking food from the moon. Adolf Bastian tells us somewhere that the Japanese see in the moon a rabbit pounding rice in a mortar. The late Hans Conon von der Gablentz, the great commentator of Ulfilas, showed me a drawing of a Chinese coin, on which was to be seen a hare sitting under a bush, and the moon above it.

Benfey, in the " Panchatantra," relates an Indian fable, according to which Indra puts the hare into the moon (Benfey, " Panch.," 1,348, 2,549). The Roman Catholic missionaries, Huc and Gabet, travelling in Central Asia, came to a city where the feast of the moon-cakes was celebrated. Their host, a disciple of Buddha, gave to each of them a cake on which the likeness of a hare and the moon was imprinted. In the Hitopadesa, the hare represents himself to the king of the elephants, as the messenger of the moon. In fact, one of the Sanskrit names of the moon is *çaçin*, " the one with the hare" (*vide* Benfey, " Sanscrit-English Dictionary," çaçin and çaça-dhara). The god of the moon is often represented sitting in a carriage drawn by two antelopes and having a hare in his hand. The natives of Ceylon also pretend to see a hare in the moon. In Saxony an old nurse told me that a hare was to be seen in the moon. Also, if a child is born with a split lip, or a so-called hare-lip, in Northern Bavaria and in Westfalia, and in the neighbourhood of Magdeburg, the nurses will ascribe it to the influence of the moon. Shakspeare evidently must have known also some of these superstitions regarding the moon, when Caliban says to Stefano, " I have seen thee in the moon !" Be this enough. It would, indeed, fill a small volume to enumerate all the various ideas each nation entertains about the moon.

|*Garubeb.*

This name of Heitsi-eibib is a mere local appellation

in use among the ǀKora of the Middle Orange River and the River of ǁHaintas. An old ǀKora at the convict station, Cape Town, told me that ǀGarubeb often died and rose again; that on his grave are strewn branches and stones; that he was a great chief, and possessed plenty of cattle. The etymology of the name does not offer great difficulty. ǀ*Garu* means *spotted, tufted.* ǀGã is grass; ǀgaru, therefore, is what grows in *tufts*, like grass. Here, in South Africa, it is a characteristic of the grass that it does not equally cover the whole ground, but that it stands about in tufts. Evidently the word ǀ*gamirob* comes from the same root, ǀ*ga*, from which ǀgarubeb, and ǀgarub, the leopard (the spotted one), derive their origin. Stars mean accordingly *the dots, the points*, those who stand *in tufts.* The myth says also that Heitsi-eibib's mother became pregnant in swallowing the juice of a certain grass. We can now either translate ǀGarubeb, *the grass-man*, or *the spotted-one.* I am, however, more inclined to adopt the latter interpretation, and that for the following reason :— In the preceding pages I have shown the identity of Heitsi-eibib with ǁKhāb, the Moon. A look at the moon's spotted face explains easily the name, ǀgarubeb, the spotted-one. Whether the ancient Khoikhoi saw in the spots of the moon a great many grass tufts, I cannot say, but it is not impossible.

Tūsib.

Tūsib is also a local name for Tsūi-ǁgoab, or, better, ǀNanub. Tū means *to rain.* *Tusib*, therefore, the Rain-giver, or the one who looks like rain, who comes from the rain—that is, the one who spreads the *green shining* colour over the earth (*vide* note in second chapter, Tūsib).

ǀGurikhoisib and ǂEiχaǀkhaǀǀnabıseb.

Like Heitsi-eibib, ǀGurikoisib, or, as he is also called, ǂEiχaǀkhaǀǀnabiseb, defends the Khoikhoi against evil-

doers, especially against the Lion. The etymology of
|Gurikhoisib offers no difficulty. |*Guri* means *single,
only, alone*. Khoi-si-b derives from the root *KHOI*,
meaning *man*; with the suffix *si* it has a more collective
meaning, like *mankind*; therefore, |Gurikhoisib, means
the only man, the first man, primitive man. Here the
worship of the Supreme Being and ancestor-worship have
become amalgamated.

The name ‡Eiχa|kha||nabiseb consists of three words
—‡eiχa (from ‡ei), brass-like, |kha, body, and ||nabiseb,
the back-bone; thus the whole name conveys the meaning: "The man whose body has a brass-coloured backbone." This is the lightning, who descends from
heaven (|homi), or from the cloud (|nanub) to the earth.
Here we have, perhaps, the explanation why the Khoikhoi
women on certain occasions anoint themselves with red
ochre, and also for the purposes of worship make marks
with red ochre (torob) on certain sacred stones and
cairns.

I remarked previously that we have reason to believe
that there was among the Khoikhoi also a period when
human sacrifices formed a part of their offerings. They
still cut off a finger. I shall not be surprised if continued
investigations corroborate the idea that the painting
of the sacred stones with red ochre was merely an act
to replace the cruel offering of human blood by a simple
symbolical ceremony. It may also be that the red
lightning, in killing a man, and thus demanding blood,
might in the commencement have led to human sacrifice;
and that the red colour of the lightning and the bloody
sacrifice together afterwards introduced the use of red
ochre or other red paint into the worship of the Khoikhoi.
I have already quoted in the second chapter from
Ludolf's "Commentary," p. 228, "Uxores solere conspergere caput dei *terra rubra.*" In place of this terra
rubra (red ochre, *tōrob*), they also use frequently the red
tannic juice of the Acacia giraffæ.

The Ostiaks, when they kill an animal, rub some of the blood on the mouths of their idols. Even this seems at length to be replaced by red paint. Thus the sacred stones in India, as Colonel Forbes Leslie has shown, are frequently ornamented with red. So also, in Congo, it is customary to daub the fetishes with red every new moon.—*Vide* Lubbock, " Origin of Civilization," p. 270.

!Urisib and !Urisis, Tsēb and Sūris.

The myth tells us that !Urisib is Heitsi-eibib's son. The root of this word is !ū, as it is still preserved in the !Ai Bushman, where it originally means the egg, and white. Certainly the word !ū served, in the second instance, to express the colour *white*, and the ostrich egg, of which the contents are eaten, of which the shell serves as a water-cask, and of which the Bushman makes his ornaments, is *white*. Here in our myth is !Urisis, the Sun, the white one; but as the shape of the *Sun* is round, and as its colour is white, it is not unlikely that it was originally called *the egg par excellence*. According to the Khoikhoi custom of giving the son the name of the mother, the son of !Urisis was !*Urisib*—*i.e.*, Tsēb, the day, the daylight. !Urisis, the white one, however, is again called *Suris*, the Sun. Suris gives the root *su*, to broil, to be hot; Soris or Suris, therefore, means the broiling-one, the heating-one, the inflaming-one. Derivative forms from *sū* are *sāi*, to boil, *sūs*, the pot, or the boiling instrument. *Sureb* or *soreb* (masc.), *sores* (fem.), the lover, the sweetheart, the one who is inflamed—viz., with love, or who inflames with love; *Soregu*, to court, to fall in love, to be in love.

It is now obvious that !Urisis is Soris, the wife of Heitsi-eibib Tsūi||goab, the Dawn, and that the son of this marriage bond is !Urisib—*i.e.*, Tsēb, the Day, or Daylight. The etymology of the word *tsē* is very obscure, and will never be unveiled. I have searched in vain for a satisfactory explanation, and, failing in this, I addressed

Mr. Krönlein, a missionary who pretends to have some knowledge of the Khoikhoi. He told me that he derives *tse* from *gei*, to grow, to develop. This is quite unscientific, as there is not a single instance in the Khoikhoi idioms of the *g* changing into *ts*. It seems that the original root is quite lost, and so is its meaning. I shall, however, make some suggestions of my own, that perhaps may lead those who still labour among the Khoikhoi on some track. We have numerous instances in Khoikhoi that *ia* contracts into *e;* and we have also the fact that *ts* has worn off into *s;* again, we have the instance that *e* and *i*, in forms like *bi* and *be*, or *si* and *se*, are promiscuously used. If we now reconstruct *tse* we shall get the form *tsia;* tsia then becomes *tsē* or *tsī ;* and *tsī* becomes *sī*. Now we have in Khoikhoi the verb *sī*, to come, to arrive, to approach. I have, in the analysis of the name Tsūi||goab, shown that ||goa means to come, to approach, and here we have only in tsēb another form, which in meaning is identical with ||*goab*, the approaching one— viz., day. I wish, however, to be clearly understood; this derivation is a mere suggestion, and nothing more, but I claim for it a greater possibility than one would claim for such an etymology as is offered in *tse* from *gei*.

‡Gama‡gorib.

Almost identical with ||*Gaunab*, the opponent of *Tsūi||goab*, is ‡*Gama*‡*gorib*. The etymology of this name offers great difficulty. ‡*Gama*, from the root ‡*gā*, signifies to sink down, to fall down, to drop, by sinking down to enter the ground ; but it is also transitively used to throw down, to put into the ground, to plant. ‡*Gori*, again, from the root ‡*go*, *to go to one side, to jump out of the way, to give road.* For instance, if a person meets another, the one will say to the other, ‡*go*, make room, give way, go to one side ; therefore ‡Gama‡gorib is *the one who in falling down, or throwing himself down, always moves to the side.* This is certainly nothing else but the lightning, whose nature it is never to go in a straight line, but always to go out of the original course. We previously stated that the |Guri-khoisib was also called ‡Eiχa|kha||nabiseb, and we interpreted this name with Lightning. |Gurikhoisib is a good Being, but ‡Gama‡gorib is a bad Being, and so is ||Gaunam.

We need not be surprised at such idiosyncrasies in mythology, and especially in the so-called *lower mythology.* This is only a repetition of the maxim that the religious sentiment of mankind originally saw in Nature the working of demons; and that only after a higher state of culture the idea of a good Being is developed. After the evidence produced, we must admit that the Khoikhoi mythology, although it bears in many respects comparison with the myths of Greece and Eran, must be classified with the *lower mythologies,* for the simple reason that the Khoikhoi language has not yet left the agglutinative stage.

Ghosts and Spectres—|*Hai*|*nun and Sobo-khoin.*

The ghosts and spectres are called |Hai|nun, fawn-feet, or Sobo-khoin, men of the shadow. These words are of a very simple etymology. As to fawn-foot, |Hai |nub, we also say in German, *ein fahles Gespenst* or *fahl wie ein Gespenst.*

|*Haŭ*|*gai*|*gaib,* ‡*Amab and* |*Õas.*

|Haŭ|gai|gaib and ‡Amab are also mythological persons, but their derivation is not quite clear to me. The same, |õas, the hare, which certainly has nothing to do with |oā', to mourn, as some interpreters explain it; rather it may be derived from |õ'a, to oppose, to go against somebody, to meet.

|*Khunuseti, the Pleiades.*

It is not very easy to explain the original meaning of

this name. |Gu, or |khu, or |go, and |kho, also |ko and |ku, in the various Khoikhoi idioms of Great Namaqualand, mean close, next; hence |khu or |gu, to come, to heap, to cluster, to join; |gu-khoib, the nearest man —*i.e.*, neighbour; |gu-se, adv., closely; |gure or |gore to approach the gods—*i.e.*, to pray, as we have in German, *Jemanden angehen;* in Latin, adire deos, adire regem. From this |gu or |khū we have the derivative |gunub (|khunub or |kunub), meaning both finger and reed, and also joint of the finger and joint of the reed. Thus the original meaning of finger is the one who closes himself up to the other, the one who approaches the other, the one who joins the other—*i.e.*, the join-er, the link, the branch, the twig; and speaking and thinking in the way of a primitive man or a child—nay, even in our own phraseology—are not the fingers the twigs and branches of the hand? Hence, also, a shrub-like acacia, which branches off like the fingers of the hand, is called in the plural form |kunuti and |kunuseti. Here we have the same name for the accacia and for the Pleiades, and I think we are with this in the possession of the key to unlock the original meaning of the name Pleiades. |Khunuseti, or |kunuseti, the Pleiades, mean exactly the same as the Latin Vergiliæ—that is, the stars of the offshoots, the stars of the branches (Jupiter Viminius). As we have seen in the second chapter, at the return of the Pleiades, Tsūi||goab is particularly invoked to give rain. After the rain, the earth shoots forth herbs; branches link to branches, and leaves join to leaves. This is the one explanation of |Khunuseti.

But |Khunuti is also applied in the meaning of branch, lineage, family. Thus, I once heard a man speaking of the |Khunuti—*i.e.*, families of a clan. In the Orion myths we have |Khunuseti, the Pleiades, the daughters of Tsūi||goab; and if they are the daughters, the Father's— *i.e.* Tsūi||goab's—name must have been |Khunusib. Thus, we get |Khunuseti, the *Offshoots*, the *primordia* of the Khoikhoi. Now in Khoikhoi the clan or tribe is never called after the father, but always after the mother; the same with families. Thus we have the Nama-*s*, ǃAma*s*, ǁKhau*s*, ǀGamiǂnu*s*, ǂKhaχa*s*, never Nama-*b*, &c., in the masculine form as a tribal appellation. Thus ǀKhunuseti means nothing else but primordium, *Uranfang*. This explanation is supported by the fact that the Pleiades, like Tsũiǁgoab, the All-Father of the Khoikhoi, come from the East, where the Khoikhoi say is their "*Fatherland*." Very curious to say, in Zulu we have Uthlanga—that is, reed. It is not impossible that, as so many things and customs have been adopted by the southern Bantu from the Khoikhoi, this Khoikhoi word also, ǀ*Khunusib* or ǀ*Khunuseti*, was misunderstood or, better, misinterpreted in a one-sided way, which lay nearest to the grasp of the Zulu mind; and thus ǀKhunusib Uthlanga was explained reed, while it meant offshoot. Thus it is that the Zulus say they take their origin from Uthlanga, the reed. Inquiring from the natives of Great Namaqualand the true meaning of ǀKhunub and ǀKhunuseti, I received the following explanations:—

(1.) Those who stand together.
(2.) Those who are heaped.
(3.) Those who stand together like fingers.
(4.) Those who cluster together.
(5.) The thorn-stars.

This latter explanation again brings to our mind the name the Lion gives to ǀKurikhoisib Tsũiǁgoab. He calls him ǁKhuǃnomab, Root of the Thorntree.

Now, I do not mean to say that my explanation is absolutely right, but I can at least claim as much right and notice for it as others claim for their explanation of this name. My opinion is also supported by the fact that the Khoikhoi calculate their time according to the rainy season. With the setting-in of the rains commences their year, a new turn of life. We can also now understand the meaning if it is said of Tsũiǁgoab and Heitsi-eibib

L

that they are possessed of plenty of cattle, The Pleiades in a certain sense represent a flock. Dr. Callaway correctly remarks that the meaning of Uthlanga has been lost, while the word has come down to the present generations. And it is the same with the word ǀKhunuseti. That the Namaquas have not borrowed this name from the Bantu (Herero) is quite obvious, because they have been too short a time in contact with the Herero, who, besides, have no myth about Uthlanga, and also have no clicks in their language. In ǀKora we have the form kūseti (contracted from ǀkunuseti), and in Cape Hottentot we have ǀgŏti and ǀkŭti (contracted from ǀgonoti and ǀkunuti). This confirms beyond doubt that the Khoikhoi not only had the same name for the Pleiades previous to their separation, but that, in those remote days, there already existed among them a sidereal mythology and worship. In the second chapter we saw that in George Schmidt's time, at the return of the Pleiades, the same prayer was uttered which is still annually heard among the heathen Khoikhoi of Great Namaqualand.

Among the Israelites ideas seem also to have existed which connected the Lord with the Pleiades and Orion. "Seek him," says Amos (v. 8), "that maketh the Seven Stars and Orion, and turneth the shadow of death into morning, and maketh the day dark with night: that calleth for the waters of the sea, and poureth them out upon the face of the earth: the Lord is his name."

And again, "Which maketh," says Job (ix. 9), "Arcturus, Orion, and Pleiades." And the same author (xxxix. 31) asks: "Canst thou bind the sweet influences of the Pleiades, or loose the bands of Orion?"

[This translation is not quite in accordance with the Hebrew text. It should be, "Canst thou *join* the *links* of the Pleiades?"]

It is certainly to be considered of extraordinary importance that the Pleiades and Orion are mentioned together; it cannot be merely accidental. And of the Lord the same Prophet Amos says, "It is He that buildeth His stories in heaven?" And have we not heard and seen, in the second chapter, how Tsūi||goab also buildeth his stories in heaven?

As to the connection of the Pleiades with the religious ideas of the various nations of the world, it is certainly a strange coincidence that they, or, better, the brightest of them, Alcyone, a star of the third magnitude, were considered to occupy the apparent positions of the central point round which our universe of fixed stars is revolving.

We have also to note what Max Müller says in his "Lectures on the Science of Language" (London, 1866, vol. i. 8), and especially the foot-note 5 :—" In the Oscan inscriptions of Agnone, a Jupiter Virgarius (djorei verehasioi, dat. sing.) occurs, a name which Professor Aufrecht compares with that of Jupiter, who fosters the growth of twigs (Kuhn's "Zeitschr." i. 5, 89). This explanation is more analogous to the idea of the Khoikhoi, where Tsūi||goab is invoked for rain, that the grass and bushes may grow.

Professor Max Müller certainly has his reasons for deriving πλείαδες from πλέω, but after what has been explained in the preceding pages, I think no objection could be raised as to a derivation from the form πλείων (comparative); and thus πλείαδες would mean, "those who are in a heap, those who are many." The πλείαδες, or priestesses of Zeus at Dodona, sang, "Zeus was, Zeus is, Zeus will be a great Zeus." Here the Supreme Being of the Greeks, Zeus, is also brought into connection with the Pleiades. We speak of a "Song of the Spheres" (*German, Sphärengesang*), and the Psalmist says, "The heavens declare the glory of God."

Now, why were the priestesses called πλείαδες, generally translated *pigeons*. Here, like Uthlanga and !Khunuseti, the original meaning was lost, and the word only brought down to posterity. A certain kind of pigeon was called πελειάς. Pigeons are, as Plato would say, ζῶα πολιτικά; they are always in numbers, in heaps. In the woods around the Temple of Dodona were numbers of pigeons, which were under the protection of Zeus. And when the original meaning of πλειάδες (the "heaped stars") was forgotten, the word πλεῖας (pigeon), derived also from the same root, was applied to the priestesses who sang the "Hymns of the Spheres" and were called pigeons. When this etymology was forgotten, the circumstance that at the rise of the Seven stars on the eastern horizon the shipping season commenced, the phonetical coincidence of the root of Pleiades and the word πλεῖν (to navigate) led to the new explanation, "the shipping stars." We may be almost certain that the name πλειάδες existed long before the Greeks thought of crossing the Mediterranean and the stormy Pontus Euxinus.

This explanation of mine is merely a suggestion, on which I shall be glad to learn the opinion of competent etymologists in the Indo-Germanic realm.

Conclusion.

My task so far is done. My intention was solely to produce such evidence as to prove the strong, but hitherto unjustly underrated, religious sentiment of a race of men of whom it is generally believed that they belong to the lowest of the low. Although, on the one hand, these myths must be grouped among the *lower mythology*, it does not follow that the religious sentiment expressed in them should not be strongly developed. Before the Khoikhoi called *Tsūi*‖*goab* (the Dawn), ‖*Khăb* (the moon), or *Heitsi-eibib* (Dawn tree), Gods, it was first necessary to form a clear idea of the *Godhead*. And this they have done in a most emphatical way; the name |Khūb, the Lord, the Ruler, bears testimony to that. This name was formed long before the tribes separated to migrate to the right and left, and we are correct in presuming that at that time their religious ideas were much purer than we find them now, where various circumstances have worked to accelerate their annihilation.

If religion means faith in a " Heavenly Father" who is near to his children in their troubles; if it expresses the belief in an almighty and powerful Lord, who gives rain and good seasons; if it involves the idea of a " Father of Lights, from whom cometh down every good gift and every perfect gift, with whom is no variableness, neither shadow of turning;"—if this father is an avenger, who sees everything, and punishes the bad and the criminal, and rewards the good; if religion manifests that craving of the heart after the Invisible, if not here on earth, then in a better world to see Him face to face; if it indicates a sense of human weakness and dependence on the one hand, and an acknowledgment of a Divine government on the other;—we cannot for a single moment hesitate to assign to the Khoikhoi the same place in Nature that we claim for ourselves. The great gulf which separates man from the animal kingdom is the gift to express the feelings and yearnings of our heart in articulate speech. This gift, in a very great measure, cannot be denied to the Khoikhoi.

The time has passed when we could build up science by lofty theories. What we require are positive facts. Such facts as regards the Science of Religion in reference to the Khoikhoi I have tried to produce. I only regret that they are so few, owing to the difficulty a traveller has to contend with, if he searches for those precious jewels which are the most sacred and dearest to the human heart. I shall, however, feel amply rewarded if, in the shape offered, they will be of use to the student of the Science of Religion, and if they have opened to us new avenues into the pre-historic intellectual and religious condition of the Khoikhoi. I have only produced the ore, and done my best to clean it; the student must mould it into shape. For the purpose of facilitating a better understanding, I have now and then made an excursional trip to other races, and pointed out the striking resemblances between those nations and our Khoikhoi. If, however, somebody should be induced to infer from this that I belong to that class of scholars who, for the sake of upholding some biblical dogma, grasp at such analogies, I beg herewith most emphatically to protest against any such insinuations. It has not been done to claim anthropological or ethnic relationship for the worshippers of Tsũi||goab and those of Dyaus or Jehovah or Buddha. Nothing could be more opposed to my scientific views, which in ethnological and mythological matters may be condensed in the following words—" The same objects and the same phenomena in Nature will give rise to the same ideas, whether social or mythical, among different races of mankind, in different regions, and at different times." And if this be correct, which I have no doubt it is, we have thus to explain the *psychical identity* of human nature.

I hope that these pages may be an impulse to missionaries to look deeper into the eyes of a Hottentot. Perhaps they may discover some more sparks of the primæval revelation. Missionaries, I regret to say, are so apt to treat the heathen gods as demons or evil spirits (*Abgötter, Götzen*). It is also very wrong to teach the heathen so eagerly, as is done by certain missionaries, our dogmas, and to tell them of the differences of Calvinism and Lutheranism. There is something like fanaticism in this—a zealotism which can never bear fruit. To them, also, the poet gives the warning:

> Grau, Freund, ist alle Theorie
> Und ewig grün des Lebens goldener Baum.
>
> (Grey, friend, is all theory,
> And green the golden tree of life.)

The abode of true religion—I mean of the true yearning

and craving after the Infinite—is our heart, which becomes deaf and dumb as soon as it is surrounded by the mist and clouds of dogmatism. The key-note of true religion is love—a key-note which is never touched in the fanatical controversies of our modern dogmatists.

What I have said I mean," without offence to any friends or foes." I do not pretend that my comments and inferences are absolutely infallible, so as not to admit of the opinion of others. And I shall be glad to hear such opinions, little concerned whether my own views be overthrown, as long as it will serve to solve one of the most interesting, but at the same time most difficult, problems —namely, the discovery of the Origin of Religion.

The greatest satisfaction to me, however, would be if this little book will induce my countrymen to look with a different eye at the natives, especially at the unjustly cried-down Hottentots, the gipsies of South Africa. They undoubtedly possess every disposition for social improvement, but the dearth of water in South Africa, which always compels its inhabitants to renew their wanderings, has precluded any density of population, one of the most necessary factors for the progress of civilization. We should never forget that the social condition of our Teutonic ancestors at the time of Cæsar was little better than " that of the Khoikhoi, but their language was even then Aryan in dignity." " But as the Greeks had to learn that some of these so-called barbarians possessed virtues which they might have envied themselves, so we also shall have to confess that these savages have a religion and a philosophy of life which may well bear comparison with the religion and philosophy of what we call the civilizing and civilized nations of antiquity" (Max Müller, " Hibbert Lect.," 70).

To judge from the fragments we just had before us, we can clearly see that the Khoikhoi very early, long before their separation, had an idea of the Supreme Being, whom they all invoked by the name of Tsūi-||goab, just as the name Dyaus was used among the ancestors of our own race, and has been handed down to us, to our historical times. Certain it is, also, that hand in hand came the decay of the nationality went a retrogression and decay of the religious ideas. I do not speak too boldly if I maintain that the Khoikhoi language, if its makers would only have had the necessary inducement, must have become an inflecting language. And then the intellectual vivacity of the Khoikhoi, combined with their mythopœic power, undoubtedly would have produced as charming and fanciful mythologies as we admire in the myths of Eran, Hellas, and Thule.

NOTES TO THE THIRD CHAPTER.

[1] Confer Pott: Die Sprachen vom Kaffer und Kongostamme, in *Zeitschrift der deutschen morgenländischen Gesellschaft*, ii. 5–26, 129–158. Hans Conon von der Gabelentz on the same subject in the same Proceedings, i. 241.

[2] Max Müller, " Chips," ii. 262.

[3] |Ava-khoin—*i.e.*, Redmen—is a name which the Khoikhoi often employ, chiefly in order to distinguish themselves from the much-hated black races, whom they sometimes call χ*un*, things, or more emphatically, *arin*, dogs.

[4] Theophilus Hahn, Der Hottentotische Tsũi||goab und der Indogermanische Zeus : *Zeitschrift der Gesellschaft für Erdkunde*, Berlin, 1870, p. 452.

[5] The Bushmen whom Livingstone met in the Kalihari told him that death was sleep. Similarly Arbousset tells us about the notions of the Bushmen of Basutoland, and the same idea is entertained by the |Kham Bushmen in the Northern Colony.

[6] Zuiver water is a corruption, for the correct word is "*Zypelen*," to filter.

[7] In South African Dutch the |gubib is called broekkaros, the trouser-shaped cover or skin. The word broek is Dutch, meaning trousers, and karos is a corrupt form of the Khoikhoi kho-ro-s, a diminutive form of khōb, skin, hide.—*Vide* On the Formation of Diminutives, Theoph. Hahn, "Sprache der Nama," § 20, 1.

[8] On the suffixes mi, m, bi, b, *see* Theoph. Hahn, "Sprache der Nama," p. 29.

[9] Suffix tsi, *vide* Theophilus Hahn, Beiträge zur Kunde der Hottentoten, p. 45 im *Jahresbericht des Vereins für Erdkunde*, Dresden," 1868, n. 1869, vi. and vii.

[10] *Orlam.* The meaning of this word is not quite clear. At present this word signifies in South African Dutch a shrewd, smart fellow. Thus they say, " Die kerel is banje orlam" (that fellow is very shrewd). Those Hottentot clans who left the Colony, and now live in Great Namaqualand, call themselves *Orlams*, in distinction from the aborigines, the Namaquas, and by this they mean to say that they are no longer uncivilized. If, for instance, they give a traveller a man as a servant, they say, " He is very *orlam;* he is not *baar*" (he is very handy; he is not stupid). In the North-western Colony, about the mission station Steinkopf, lives a large family of the *Orlams.* They manufacture stone pipes, and are Bastard Hottentots, who say that a trader, by the name of Orlam, came about a hundred years ago to Little Namaqualand, and afterwards stayed amongst the Namaquas and married a Hottentot girl. The truth is, that about 1720 there was a man at the Cape of the name of Orlam, who had come from Batavia. He was a trader, and visited chiefly Little Namaqualand and the Khamiesbergen. Peter Kolb, in his " Caput Bonae Spei hodiernum" (Nuremberg, 1719, p. 818), explains Orlam to be a corruption from the Malay Orang lami (old people, people who have experience—*i.e.*, shrewd people); and Baaren, he says, is a corruption of Orang bari, meaning "*new hands,*" without experience. Bari, how-

ever, is a good Dutch word, which we meet with in the various Teutonic languages; thus English, bare (barefaced, barefoot); Anglo-Saxon, bar, boer; Swedish, Danish, and German, bar; Dutch, baar; O. H. German, par; meaning uncovered, destitute, naked, raw, without anything. A. Wilmot, in his "History of the Cape Colony" (1869, p. 134), seems to have followed Kolb, because he says (1727) there were two classes of people in the service of the Company in India and at the Cape, named *Orlam-men* and *Baaren*—the former of whom consisted of well-known persons who had served for several years, and the latter of new-comers and comparative strangers, &c. Then, in a foot-note: "From a corruption of two words in the Malay language—Orang lami, an old person or acquaintance; Orang baru, a new person."

THE END.